MYTHS AND MYSTERIES

OF

WISCONSIN

I thought I knew Wisconsin . . . but I didn't know *this* Wisconsin! From Buddy Holly's bus trouble to the marital mysteries of Jefferson Davis—yep, that Jefferson Davis—Michael Bie has done a fine job of showing that we here in Wisconsin can weird it up with the best of 'em.

—**Michael Perry,** author of *Population: 485* and *The Clodhopper Monologues*

"As a native Badger I was conceived at Little Bohemia. My grandmother visited Ms. Van Hoof. I was awakened by Leo Burt's bomb when a senior in high school. So believe me when I vouch for the charm of Mr. Bie's wry take on the people, places and events that make Wisconsin north of normal. As fine a Wisconsin treat as a squeaky curd."

—**John Roach,** columnist, *Madison Magazine*

"Myths and Mysteries of Wisconsin will fascinate non-fiction enthusiasts—everyone from history buffs to reality show fans—with its true stories of government scandals, grisly murders, and alien abductions—with some rock and roll thrown in for good measure."

—**Kitty Dunn,** "Jonathon and Kitty in the Morning," WMMM, 105.5 FM

MYTHS AND MYSTERIES SERIES

MYTHS AND MYSTERIES

OF
WISCONSIN

TRUE STORIES
OF THE UNSOLVED AND UNEXPLAINED

MICHAEL BIE

Guilford, Connecticut

All photos by Michael Bie unless otherwise noted.

Project editor: Lauren Brancato
Layout: Justin Marciano
Map by Melissa Baker © Morris Book Publishing, LLC

Library of Congress Cataloging-in-Publication Data is available on file.

ISBN 978-0-7627-6983-4

Printed in the United States of America

10 9 8 7 6 5 4 3 2

CONTENTS

WISCONSIN

INTRODUCTION

There's a scenic road hugging the banks of the historic Fox River as it winds its way south of Green Bay. If not for the road's odd name, Lost Dauphin, one of the longtime mysteries of Wisconsin might be largely forgotten. How did the story of the "Lost Dauphin," the young prince of King Louis XVI and Marie Antoinette who supposedly was smuggled into exile following the French Revolution, make its way from the Bastille to Brown County? Did the prince, heir to the throne of France, really live in a cabin overlooking the Fox River? There was compelling evidence to suggest the man claiming royal blood was an impostor, yet he was the subject of books and articles and feted among the high society of his time. For more than 150 years it was generally believed Eleazor Williams was a fake, a poser. But we weren't quite certain. It was in this slight and seductive window of possibility that Eleazor Williams lived and excelled in his day, fabricating a mystery that long outlived him. The truth did not surface until 2000.

The case of Joe Davis, a Menominee Indian from northeast Wisconsin who fought against the South in the Civil War, also focuses on the question of true identity. To the Menominee people, there is no mystery about Joe Davis—it's a matter of tribal record. Perhaps the larger mystery concerns how the birth of Joe

Davis may have turned the accepted history of two substantial American figures on its head.

Sure, Wisconsin is best known for dairy products, fermented malt beverages, sausages, and a certain pro football team (things best enjoyed at the same time, incidentally). There's no myth or mystery in that. Looking for the best cheese in the world? We got it. But beyond the rolling farm fields and scenic lakes, the vast northern forests and working class cities, you'll find no shortage of intrigue, of stories cast in shadows and various shades of gray.

It was deep in the North Woods that rock-and-roll pioneer Buddy Holly suffered the brunt of a Wisconsin winter, leading to a fateful decision days later. From Marinette came a simple working man who commanded the world's stage in the fall of 1986—a man who has struggled under the weight of the myth surrounding him ever since.

In Milwaukee, Wisconsin's "Beer Town," surveillance and undercover work shed some light on the shadowy world of mob boss Frank Balistrieri, yet he escaped prosecution from the Feds' most serious charge: that he was the most dangerous man in Milwaukee, responsible for the violent deaths of at least a half-dozen people, as well as for arson and bombings against those who defied him.

In La Crosse, the leafy college town resting below the bluffs along the Mississippi River valley, the problems associated with the longstanding tradition of that river city spawned an unprecedented wave of panic just a few years ago. Another scenic location,

Waupaca, best known today for its chain of lakes, for decades was a town in turmoil, suffering "a horrid dread" resulting from the brutal death of the town banker. The ring of suspects who ultimately were acquitted for the crime included several prominent citizens of the day. It's a mystery that will linger for the ages, fraught with theories about what happened that frightful night.

The facts and fictions of Captain Dan Seavey's life are so intermingled at this point in time it's hard to discern the truth. We do know this: Scale down the tall tales and Seavey looms large. He was the only man charged with piracy on the Great Lakes; that alone deserves a place of standing.

Joe Simonton was best known for playing Santa Claus in Eagle River's holiday parade until he became the center of Wisconsin's most famous story about close encounters with aliens. The work of backwoods miracle healer John Till generated legions of devoted followers in the early 1900s for reasons that remain fuzzy at best. Byron Kilbourn was a founding father of Milwaukee and a player in the state's constitutional convention, a big man and a big shot who wasn't above stooping to new lows in an age "fogged with political trickery and legislative chicanery."

Two Wisconsin women claimed visits from the Virgin Mary. One case brought all the rebuke the local Catholic diocese could muster, while the other was decreed "worthy of belief" more than a century later.

Chief among Badger State intrigues is the fate of Leo Burt, one of the four radicals responsible for the bombing of the University of Wisconsin Madison's Sterling Hall in 1970 that killed a young physicist, landing Burt on the FBI's Most Wanted list. After exhausting every possible lead to his whereabouts across the span of the past forty years, authorities can only conclude that Leo Burt remains certifiably, unquestionably, inexplicably missing. Leo Burt sightings are among the many pastimes in Wisconsin, and, who knows, it could very well be him standing there. Look beyond the bucolic farm fields and placid lakes and you'll find a state with a compelling history of myths and mysteries.

CHAPTER 1

Holy(?) Apparitions

On the arduous four-mile walk to a grist mill near her family's homestead, a sack of wheat balanced on her head, Adele Brise noticed a woman standing between two trees in the remote frontier of northeast Wisconsin. The October landscape, having just lost its brilliant autumn colors, was beginning to assume shades of brown and gray, making the appearance of the strange woman all the more unsettling—she was dressed in a brilliant white dress. Brise stopped in fear at the sight of the woman, who slowly vanished, leaving only a mist in her wake.

The twenty-seven-year-old Brise shared the story with her parents when she returned home that day.

The following Sunday on her walk to church, accompanied by two others, Brise again froze at the sight of the woman in the same location. "There's that lady again," she said, noticeably shaken. Her companions saw nothing.

Brise related her experience to Father William Verhoef after Mass that day. If it were a heavenly messenger, he counseled, it

SACRED CROSS
UNDER THY SHADOW
I REST AND HOPE

SISTER
MARIE ADELE
JOSEPH BRICE
DIED
JULY 5 1896
AT THE AGE OF 66

Brise gravesite, Champion, Wis. ("Brise" misspelled on marker.)

would not harm her and she should ask what the woman desired of her. Another member of the congregation agreed to walk with Adele and the two others on the eleven-mile journey back to the Brise homestead.

As they approached the spot between the two trees, Adele fell to her knees, trembling.

"In God's name, who are you and what do you want of me?"

The others watched in silence for a moment.

"Adele, who is it?" asked one of the women.

"Why can't we see her as you do?" asked another.

Adele began weeping.

"What more can I do, dear lady?" Brise asked.

Another moment passed.

"But how shall I teach them when I know so little myself?" she wondered aloud.

Adele Brise was born into a Catholic family in the Belgian province of Brabant in 1831. One of four children to Lambert and Marie Brise, young Adele reportedly made a promise to enter a Belgian religious order in her homeland. As fate should have it, the Brise family was among the wave of Belgian immigrants drawn to northeast Wisconsin for the abundance of forest land in the 1850s, an area that became the largest concentration of Belgian immigrants in the nation. For four years Adele accepted the rigors of pioneer life while never abandoning her religious aspirations.

It was 1859 when Brise experienced the apparitions of the Virgin Mary. The Catholic Church defines an apparition as an appearance of Jesus Christ, the Virgin Mary, or one of the saints. An appearance may include a message for the person who sees the apparition. There are only twelve Church-approved sightings. The most well-known apparitions of the Virgin Mary are Our Lady of Guadalupe, Mexico, in the year 1531; Lourdes, France in 1858; and Fatima, Portugal in 1917. The Church has dismissed countless other claims of apparitions.

Today Wisconsin is home to one of the rare sanctioned sightings—and one of the more sensational unsanctioned sightings.

On October 9, 1859, moments after Adele Brise recovered from the vision, she explained to her companions what she had seen: It was the Blessed Virgin, clothed in white, with a yellow sash around her waist, the dress falling to her feet in graceful folds, a crown of stars encircling her head, and long, golden, wavy hair to her shoulders. A light shone around her. She was indescribably beautiful.

When Brise saw the third apparition on her way home from Mass that Sunday afternoon, she did what the priest had instructed.

"In God's name, who are you and what do you want of me?"

"I am the Queen of Heaven, who prays for the conversion of sinners, and I wish you to do the same. You received Holy

Communion this morning, and that is well, but you must do more. Make a general confession, and offer Communion for the conversion of sinners. If they do not convert and do penance, my Son will be obliged to punish them."

When the others asked Brise who she saw and why they couldn't see, the apparition responded to Brise, "Blessed are they that believe without seeing."

"What more can I do, dear Lady?" Brise asked.

"Gather the children in this wild country and teach them what they should know for salvation."

"But how shall I teach them when I know so little myself?" Brise responded.

"Teach them their catechism, how to sign themselves with the sign of the Cross, and how to approach the sacraments. That is what I wish you to do. Go and fear nothing. I will help you."

According to Brise, Mary lifted her hands as though giving a blessing and slowly vanished.

Not surprisingly, reactions were mixed when the news spread about Adele Brise's visions of the Virgin Mary. Her father constructed a small chapel at the spot of the vision. Others considered her to be delusional. Members of the Catholic hierarchy were skeptical. Brise embarked on a lifelong mission to catechize children living in the region as instructed, she believed, crisscrossing the region at a time when there was a dearth of priests. The work required laborious travel through rugged and unsettled terrain, and in all manner of weather. She established a Catholic school and a community of Franciscan nuns next to the chapel.

A steady stream of pilgrims—and charlatans—made their way to the site near Champion, Wisconsin, in southern Door County. The Church grew increasingly unhappy, at one point placing an interdict on the chapel and the school and threatening Brise with excommunication, though she had nothing to do with the unsavory activities occurring there. With every challenge from her church, Brise's sincerity, zeal, and steadfast teaching of the children of the frontier redeemed her in the eyes of the authorities.

The year 1871 was notable in northeast Wisconsin for the drought experienced throughout the summer and fall. On October 8 fire struck the community of Peshtigo on the west shore of Green Bay, claiming 2,500 lives in what remains the worst wildfire in the nation's history. The conflagration created its own atmosphere, resulting in a hurricane that carried fire thirty miles east over the bay to ignite parts of southern Door County. As the holocaust struck near Champion, Brise and others nearby fled to the chapel for protection. After the fire burned itself out, the morning light revealed the entire area was destroyed except for five acres surrounding the shrine.

Brise died in 1896. Her last words, said to her Franciscan sisters, were, "I rejoiced in what was said to me. We shall go into the house of the Lord." She is buried near the shrine where she experienced the apparitions thirty-seven years earlier. The place quietly served as a destination for pilgrims over the years, often unknown even to residents living in the area.

Maybe the low-key atmosphere associated with the Champion shrine can be attributed to its overshadowing by the sensational modern-day claim of Marian apparitions reported in central Wisconsin.

Mary Ann Van Hoof, a slight, plainspoken farmwife who resided with her husband and seven children near Necedah, awoke one night in the fall of 1949 with a feeling that somebody was in her room. According to Van Hoof, standing before her was the Virgin Mary, wearing a cream-colored dress with a light blue cloak adorned with stars on the trim. A thin veil covered the figure's head and Van Hoof said she could see that Mary was a blonde. Frightened, Van Hoof pulled the sheets over her head.

Months later, on the evening of Good Friday, 1950, Van Hoof noticed that the crucifix on her wall was glowing. A voice said, "I will come again when the grass is green and the leaves are on the trees, but not in this room."

Van Hoof said it was the most beautiful voice she had ever heard.

On May 28, with the fields and trees in full bloom, Van Hoof stepped to the door of her farmhouse to call the kids to dinner when she saw a flash of light.

"I looked up and out through the door and saw a blue mist behind some trees, then the vision became the figure of our

Mother. She was so radiant and beautiful an artist couldn't paint her to justice."

The apparition instructed her to build a shrine. Obediently, Van Hoof erected a statue of the Virgin Mary in the middle of the four ash trees. Word spread that this was another Fatima (the Portuguese town made famous for the Marian appearances reported in 1917) and soon, aided by something not available in Adele Brise's time—modern media—members of clergy, believers, and the simply curious began flocking to the shrine.

The Holy Mother's message, as relayed through Van Hoof, was simple: "Pray, pray, pray, pray hard."

The Catholic Diocese of La Crosse sent representatives to speak with Van Hoof and concluded the claims were "spurious and highly questionable," the product of Van Hoof's "unstable emotionalism and misguided zeal." Bishop John Treacy prohibited religious services at the site.

Undaunted, Van Hoof announced that another appearance would take place August 15 on the Catholic holy day known as the Assumption of the Blessed Virgin Mary. Van Hoof was now generating headlines near and far. More than 175,000 copies of a pamphlet written by believers were circulated throughout the country. Anticipation mounted through the hot summer of 1950.

Bishop Treacy did his best to stem the inexorable tide of people heading to Necedah. Van Hoof's claims were extremely doubtful in nature, he reiterated. "Stay at home and pray the rosary there."

By the morning of August 15, four vast farm fields were filled with more than fifteen thousand vehicles bearing license plates from at least thirty-eight states. The roadways were choked with visitors. Hundreds of buses had been chartered. Special trains rolled into Necedah every twenty minutes.

Just before noon, Van Hoof, her husband, children, and mother walked from the house and knelt at the shrine.

"An impressive hush fell over the throng," reported the *Necedah Republican*. The crowd was estimated at one hundred thousand. "There was literally not a human sound."

Van Hoof prayed for ten minutes, then addressed the crowd, repeating what she claimed she had just been told by the Blessed Virgin: "All religions must work together, not in jealousy and hatred, but in love. Love thy neighbor." Overcome with emotion, Van Hoof retreated to her farmhouse, a delegation from the La Crosse diocese following her inside for an interview.

Another "vision day" was held in October. The crowd was significantly smaller, but thousands still came. This gathering was bit more dramatic. As she held her crucifix aloft, the sun broke through the clouds, causing a stir in the crowd.

Van Hoof continued for decades to come, allegedly suffering from stigmata and seeing miniature angels and saints in trees and sitting on fence posts. Her messages became increasingly bizarre. She urged followers to enlist for a spaceship captained by an ancient man named Alex who would take followers into the center of the Earth after the Apocalypse. She claimed thirty thousand priests were spies for the Soviet Union. Not surprisingly, the Church drew a hard line, declaring, "All claims regarding supernatural revelations and visions made by Mrs. Van Hoof are false. Furthermore, all public and private religious worship connected with these false claims is prohibited." In the 1970s the La Crosse diocese excommunicated anyone associating with the shrine.

Van Hoof died in 1984. A small group of followers carried on. "It is well known that there's a certain survivalist mentality with regard to the shrine," said a diocese spokesman in 1998. "I think there are certain elements that are cultic in nature."

An occasional visitor can still be seen praying at the shrine, but the days when tens of thousands of people made their way to Necedah are long gone, faded like the weather-beaten statues dotting the property.

Van Hoof's shrine lies in stark contrast to the shrine established by Adele Brise, where the bishops in the Green Bay diocese became supportive and the annual masses conducted on the holy day of the Assumption of the Blessed Virgin Mary drew modest crowds. No bishop in the Green Bay diocese, however, had taken the steps to make an official declaration of the Champion site. In 2009 Bishop David Ricken initiated a formal investigation conducted by three church experts. At the heart of the probe were concerns if there was enough evidence to support a judgment in favor of the supernatural character of the events. According to one of the experts, a lack of hard information did "not invalidate the overall impression of coherence between event and consequences, personality of the seer and commitment to the mission received, the comparability between this event and similar recognized apparitions, and challenges of the historical context and responses given."

The Church's decision to sanction Brise's vision came in December 2010, which put the shrine on the map. It was with "moral certainty," the bishop's decree stated, "that the events, apparitions, and locutions given to Adele Brise in October of 1859 do exhibit the substance of supernatural character, and I do hereby approve these apparitions as worthy of belief (although not obligatory) by the Christian faithful."

It was the first Church-validated apparition in the United States. While no one can actually prove a supernatural occurrence, it was noted, other factors are considered such as the subsequent spiritual benefits in the lives of people and of the character of the seer. Once again, just as it was in her day, the work of Adele Brise was the most compelling evidence. "She went all over this area," Bishop Ricken said, "and visited the homes that were scattered far and wide. She walked most of the time, and she'd spend several days with the children teaching them the catechism and talking with the parents about their faith. She really had an evangelistic spirit and lived that out, not just immediately after the message, but her whole life long."

Ricken also noted "countless stories of answered prayers," including "what many call miracles," among those who had prayed for help at the shrine.

The decree resulted in a flood of media attention and people making the pilgrimage to northeast Wisconsin. The number of visitors grew tenfold, with as many as eight hundred people a day visiting the site today.

"The turnout has been incredible," said Bishop Ricken. "It's been a wonderful gift to the diocese. So many people are coming, and there are all kinds of reports of answered prayers and healings continuing."

For the faithful, the only mystery is whether the modest shrine in Champion will become the next Lourdes.

CHAPTER 2

Waukaukaummahaut: Son of the Southern President

The curious tale of Joe Davis's life starts at its end. When Davis died in 1933, purportedly at the age of ninety-five, the lifelong resident of northeast Wisconsin, Civil War veteran, and Menominee Indian was appropriately memorialized—albeit with a discrepancy about which day he died (the correct day was Wednesday)—by the local newspaper, the *Shawano Leader*. Titled "Last Veteran of Civil War Dies Monday," the obituary read:

> Joe J. Davis, the last Civil War veteran of the Menominee tribe, died in the morning of Wednesday, April 5, at his home in Keshena. He was 95 years old, having been born in 1838, and was one of the oldest residents of the reservation.
>
> He is survived by a son, Paul, and several grandchildren. His second wife preceded him in death several months ago, and a relative of hers has been acting as a housekeeper for him. For some time the old man has been very feeble, and about a year

ago he became partially blind. He has always been somewhat hard of hearing.

The death of this aged Indian brings forth a host of recollections on the part of those who have lived in this region for many years and are acquainted with its picturesque history. He not only was the witness of many important historical events and the transition of this country from a wilderness, but he had the unique distinction of being the son of Jefferson Davis, the father of the Confederacy. This fact, while being known by several persons on the reservation and by several old-time residents of this community, has sometimes been disputed, but there are enough people acquainted with the facts to prove conclusively that he was indeed the son of the southerner.

Before he became leader of the rebellion of the south, Jefferson Davis was a soldier in the U.S. Army and was stationed for some time at Prairie du Chien, Wisconsin. Later he was transferred to Fort Howard, formerly located in Green Bay. One of his colleagues in the Army was Captain William Powell, who became closely identified with the history of this region.

While stationed at Fort Howard the two officers took Indian wives, buying them from their parents, as was quite a common custom in those days and carried no social stigma. Joe Davis was the child of this Indian wife. Captain Powell had two daughters who still reside on the reservation.

Southerners who regard Davis on a par with Washington and Lincoln and other national heroes dislike to place any weight in this story, but it has long been generally known. Charles Brooks of Shawano, who lived for a long time on the reservation and knew Captain Powell, is one of those familiar with the facts.

Joe Davis came to the reservation here when his tribe was moved by the government. There were several tribes of Menominees, but they were scattered around and the government wished to get them in one place to administer their affairs more efficiently. Consequently the government made a treaty with them, giving them the land in the present reservation considering that it was far enough away from civilization and unfit enough for farming so that the Indian would not be molested and would feel at home. Joe Davis has always lived there, coming to town occasionally to get his war pension and to do some trading. For some time, however, he had hardly been able to get around and consequently was an infrequent visitor.

Funeral services will be held at the Catholic Mission church in Keshena.

Let's make sure we have this right: Jefferson Davis was the father of more than the Confederacy? As a young man he took an Indian wife in Wisconsin and fathered a child who grew up to fight against his father in the Civil War? The story begs these questions and more, not the least of which is: Is this true?

It is quite possible, though it must be noted there are inconsistencies in the reported version—more on that in a moment.

As the *Shawano Leader* stated, the life and death of Joe Davis opened a Pandora's box of intrigue concerning the "picturesque history" of the territory in the 1830s, mysteries not only involving Jefferson Davis, the future president of the Confederacy, but also Zachary Taylor, the future president of the United States. The story of Joe Davis casts an entirely new light on the relationship between these important figures, turning the commonly accepted history of Davis and Taylor on its head. And the story takes more twists and turns than a modern made-for-cable TV melodrama—only this story is better because it's real.

The common version of the story starts with this: "I'll be damned if another daughter of mine will marry into the army."

The concerned father who only wanted the best for his daughter served as commander of Fort Crawford in Prairie du Chien. Colonel Zachary Taylor would become the nation's twelfth president, but before that, in the 1830s, his primary concern was for his daughter.

On the other hand, Sarah Knox Taylor, "Knoxie," only wanted to be with the love of her life, the dashing Lieutenant Jefferson Davis, destined to serve as the president of the Confederate States of America, who served under Colonel Taylor in Prairie du Chien.

Small world, isn't it?

Zachary Taylor, a career military man, commanded Fort Crawford in the early 1830s. Jefferson Davis was no slouch either, having graduated from West Point in 1828 at age twenty.

Portrait of Jefferson Davis, president of the Confederate States of America, in Union uniform (Whi-73377).

Taylor's family, consisting of his wife, five daughters, and a son, lived on the compound. It should be noted here that Prairie du Chien was a rugged, remote, and—yes—lonely outpost in the old Northwest Territory.

The problem was that, as daughters of a career military man living in a godforsaken wilderness outpost, the Taylor girls had but two choices: Date a soldier, or don't date at all. The old man pretty much eliminated choice number one.

"Knowing the hardships of a military wife," reads his official White House biography, "Taylor opposed his daughters' marrying career soldiers."

Thus Colonel Taylor would not allow Sarah to marry his adjutant, Lieutenant Davis.

Heck, a case could be made that Zachary Taylor didn't want Jeff Davis looking at his daughter. Seems Davis was dispatched time and time again for duty far from the fort, logging in northern Wisconsin, busting squatters in Illinois (they almost killed him in a mine shaft), and pursuing defiant Indians throughout the territory. His most notable service came when the Indian chieftain Blackhawk was captured and placed in Davis's charge. It is said that the heart of the Indian captive was won by the kind treatment he received from the young officer who held him prisoner.

When Davis was at the fort, Taylor insisted on being present at all socials when the lovebirds might have an opportunity to mingle. Imagine having the man known as "Ol'

Rough & Ready" give you the evil eye at the Friday night mixer. Fun.

Still, the young couple's love grew, as did the tension between Colonel Taylor and Lieutenant Davis. When Davis sided against his commander on a minor point of order during a court martial case, well, he quickly found himself promoted to the Southwest Territory in 1833.

But time and distance could not extinguish the flames of passion begun in Prairie du Chien, "prairie of the dog" as named by French fur traders.

This nugget survived in Jefferson Davis's papers, written December 19, 1834:

[Your] kind, dear letter, I have kissed it often and it has driven many mad notions from my brain. Sarah whatever I may have hereafter I will ascribe to you. Neglected by you I should be worse than nothing and if the few good qualities I possess shall under your smiles yield a fruit it will be yours as the grain is the husbandman's. Shall we not soon meet to part no more? Oh! how I long to lay my head upon that breast which beats in unison with my own, to turn from the sickening sight of worldly duplicity and look in those eyes so eloquent of purity and love.

Yuck. No wonder most of his other letters were destroyed.

Obviously the guy had it good (bad?) for Sarah. That's probably why Davis announced he was leaving the military in

1835. Knowing the starry-eyed couple could and would reunite, Zachary Taylor finally consented to marriage. Jefferson Davis and Sarah Taylor married June 17, 1835. Davis resigned his commission two weeks later.

The new couple moved to Mississippi to start their life together on a small plantation. In a sentimental letter to Prairie du Chien, Sarah said she imagined her mother skimming milk in the cellar or feeding the chickens.

Less than three months after her wedding, Sarah was dead from malaria. Davis mourned for years. He didn't remarry for a decade.

Thirteen years after Sarah's death, in 1848, Davis was given command of a regiment of Mississippians in the Mexican War. He served with distinction under—you guessed it—his former father-in-law.

At this point the history becomes murky. One version says the men, each carrying long-held sorrow over Sarah's death, reconciled their relationship. The other version says Davis saved Taylor's hide in the battle of Buena Vista through his skilled command and snatched victory from the jaws of defeat. Davis was wounded during the battle but remained on the field until victory was in hand. It is thought Taylor was obliged to drop the hard feelings and give his former son-in-law some respect.

Then politics intervened. Following the Mexican war, Taylor was elected president, and Davis was appointed to the US Senate.

Even though he was the owner of one hundred slaves, Taylor, ever the dutiful military man, opposed secession. He hadn't risked his neck all those years in the military to see the Union break apart.

"In February 1850 President Taylor had held a stormy conference with southern leaders who threatened secession," according to White House history. "He told them that if necessary to enforce the laws, he personally would lead the army. Persons 'taken in rebellion against the Union, he would hang . . . with less reluctance than he had hanged deserters and spies in Mexico.'"

Meanwhile, the second Mrs. Davis became a good friend of Mrs. Taylor, Sarah's mother, often calling on her at the White House.

We'll never know what might have happened between the two men as the nation headed toward civil war. Taylor died unexpectedly in 1851 after a brief illness. As he was fading, Davis and his second wife helped keep vigil at his bedside.

Davis, of course, went on to become the one and only president of the ill-fated Confederacy. One of his generals was Richard Taylor, "little Dickie" as he was known in the Wisconsin days, the younger brother of Sarah, and the only son of the man who threatened to hang secessionists personally.

End of story, right?

Not even close. The mystery of Joe Davis complicates matters considerably. The *Shawano Leader* article stated Jefferson

Davis took his Indian wife while stationed at Fort Howard in Green Bay. According to the members of the Menominee Nation, Davis had multiple children with his Indian wife named Wyno.

Certainly the news of this arrangement would have made its way to Fort Crawford when Lieutenant Davis was reassigned to Prairie du Chien, considering the forts shared personnel and were the hubs of civilization in the territory. (One can only imagine the ultimate drama in which a woman with small children shows up at the compound gate asking for Lieutenant Davis.) Zachary Taylor's refusal to allow Sarah to marry, as well as the apparent tension between him and Davis, takes an entirely different direction in consideration of this.

In Wisconsin in the decades following the 1830s it was often rumored that young Jeff Davis was something less than an officer and a gentleman. Some of this should be attributed to the fact that Davis was vilified throughout the North because of his part in the Civil War. Here's an example, as written by the *Wisconsin State Journal* in 1871, six years after the war: "This unrepentant old traitor has all the impudence of an ex-slaveholder and defeated, defiant rebel. He is a fanatic, a selfish, jealous, narrow minded man. A wretch so utterly ungrateful, so shameless, so given over to the devil, has never before been known in our history."

In a pioneer retrospective written in 1895, the Honorable Joseph T. Mills tells of his early days tutoring Zachary Taylor's children at Fort Crawford.

"The heartbroken father," Mills said of Zachary Taylor, "knew Davis as a professional libertine, unprincipled and incapable of sincere affection for Knox unless he coveted the money to which she was heir."

Ouch. The Taylors, he continued, "were reticent and lonely as if oppressed by some deep family secret, not to be disclosed to a stranger."

Then Mills takes his shot.

"Anthropologists have traced Jefferson Davis' descendents among the papooses that some years since rolled, laughed and tumbled on the mats of some doting Winnebago, Sioux or Chippewa matron, of whom she is now proud, for she has enriched and diversified posterity by the new and noisy tribe of Davis."

While it's clear that Zachary Taylor didn't want his daughters marrying into the military, could it be that the deep family secret—really not much of a secret it turns out, at least not in Wisconsin—contributed to misgivings over his beloved Knoxie marrying Jefferson Davis?

Joseph J. Davis appears in US census data as having been born "about 1838," making him ninety-five years old at the time of his death in 1933, as the *Shawano Leader* reported. The newspaper didn't realize it, but Davis's age would discredit the claim that he was the son of Jefferson Davis, who was sent packing far from Wisconsin in 1833, five years before Joe Davis's birth.

There are plausible explanations for the discrepancy. It is possible that Joe Davis never knew his birth date. Native

American calendars are different from traditional calendars, and they varied among tribes and regions. Census information getting confused in translation between languages was commonplace, too. According to the Menominee, he was ninety-five "as far as his relatives could surmise."

If Joe Davis had been born in 1833 or earlier, he would have been at least one hundred years old at the time of his death, which is not out of the realm of possibility.

We do know that Joe Davis was part of two companies of Menominee Indians who volunteered to fight for the Union in the Civil War, most of whom could not speak English. Names such as Kahwahtahwahpao (Lookaround) and Payyewahsit (Snowflake) fill the company rolls. Some mixed their English and Menominee names. Davis also went by Waukaukaummahaut. He was mustered-in August 1862 into Company K of the 22nd Regiment. According to the Menominee people, Davis also used a pseudonym throughout his service, a Menominee name understood only by his brethren and meaning this: I am the Son of the President of the South. The name itself has been lost.

Among the Menominee Nation, of which members of the Davis clan still reside, the story of Jefferson Davis's marriage and abandonment of Wyno and his children is true, a matter of tribal record.

Short of DNA testing among the remains of the two men, which is not going to happen, the mystery will endure for the ages.

CHAPTER 3

The Lost Prince

In 1841, Prince de Joinville of France was touring Canada and the United States to retrace routes used by French explorers and missionaries generations earlier. One of his planned stops was Green Bay, Wisconsin, an area that figured prominently in the days of New France. The prince traveled through the Straits of Mackinac aboard the steamer *Columbia*, soliciting local information from fellow travelers regarding history and culture, or the news of the day. He arrived in Green Bay and disembarked with a local resident named Eleazor Williams, an Episcopal minister who had resettled the Oneida Indian tribe to the area years before but had since fallen from grace among both the Oneidas and his church. The prince met with Williams at Green Bay's Astor Hotel to discuss Indian affairs.

Emerging from that meeting was not Eleazor Williams, local minister, but Louis XVII, heir to the throne of France.

Eleazor Williams's lineage is, and was in his day, clear. He just hated to admit it. His great-grandmother, Eunice Williams,

Portrait of Eleazor Williams (Whi-3021).

was well known for having been taken captive with her family in the violent raid against the Massachusetts settlement of Deerfield in 1704. The other captives in the raid were returned to New England, including the surviving members of the Williams family, except Eunice, who elected to stay with the Indians in Canada and eventually married.

Eunice's great-grandson Eleazor, a Mohawk Indian, grew up in the St. Regis tribe near Lake Champlain. Thanks to his connections with the prominent Williams clan of Massachusetts, young Eleazor was afforded the opportunity to attend English schools in the early 1800s.

According to his biographers, from an early age Williams was prone to downplaying his Indian identity by spinning all varieties of fabrications. At one point he created a grandfather who was an English surgeon, another time it was a French grandfather of royal blood. As early as 1807, when he was a young adult, he toyed with the idea of acting like a French nobleman, wearing a tinsel badge and calling himself Count de Lorraine.

Eleazor served admirably in an American ranger unit during the War of 1812, using his Indian contacts to gather intelligence on British troop movements. He was wounded slightly and commended by his officers. Eleazor being Eleazor, that wasn't enough. Later he told of being a colonel (at age twenty-five) and commanding the units that turned the tide in a pivotal battle of the war.

In 1815, Williams was confirmed into the Episcopal Church and began working as a religious teacher and catechist among the Oneida Indians of New York. His fluency in the Oneida language, similar to his own Mohawk, combined with his personal charm, produced dramatic results in converting many of the Oneidas. Soon Williams began to envision a grand confederacy of Indian nations living in the Wisconsin territory . . . a kingdom in which he would figure prominently, naturally.

Led by Williams in 1822, the Oneida Indians began moving to a tract of land west of Green Bay. A year later he married the daughter of a prominent resident who brought into the marriage 4,800 acres of prime land located along the banks of the Fox River. He was ordained a deacon in 1826.

Things were going well for the preacher. He held sway over his small flock, the beginnings of an empire as he saw it, and lived comfortably on his wife's land high above the Fox River, which served as the main thoroughfare through the territory, an ideal location to spin his fantasies for unsuspecting folks traveling the waterway. He became a frequent, all too frequent, dinner guest among the officers at Fort Howard. For fun—he just couldn't help himself—he made up stories about his wife's lineage, describing her as "a distant relative of the king of France from whom he has been honored with several splendid gifts and honors, among the rest a golden cross and star."

"Priest Williams" was becoming a little too content, neglecting his pastoral duties. By 1832 there was unrest in the valley. The Oneidas came to view him as an opportunist and dumped him as their spiritual leader. By 1842 the bishop barred Williams from representing the Episcopal Church in Wisconsin.

As one proverb says, idle hands are the devil's workshop. One biographer believes Williams delusions of grandeur accelerated with "his fall from the dizzy height he had soared to in his dreams, as despot of an Indian empire."

Williams began his second career, one for which he had trained his entire life: a fake.

The fate of Louis XVII, the ten-year-old royal heir to the throne imprisoned during the French Revolution, was one of the great mysteries of its day. Speculation swirled that the young prince, the dauphin, who reportedly died in 1795, had been smuggled into exile instead.

Pretenders to the throne began popping up all over Europe and North America in the 1800s. One man in Holland, Karl Wilhelm Naundorff, was buried in 1845 with the epitaph, "Here lies Louis XVII, King of France."

Williams was in New York when he read of the French prince's North American tour. Imagine the great pretender's pulse quickening when he read that the prince would be visiting Green Bay. Thus, when the steamship carrying the prince docked at Mackinac, the eager Eleazor Williams was apparently waiting to board the boat.

The prince asked the *Columbia*'s captain for any people knowledgeable about the Green Bay area, as was customary. The captain introduced the prince to Eleazor Williams, who just happened to be aboard. Williams also had an audience with the prince later at the Astor Hotel in Green Bay. They primarily discussed the Indian tribes living in the area.

But Williams couldn't help himself from fabricating an entirely different story. According to Williams, the prince summoned him, and when the two were introduced "there was a great agitation in his face and manner—a slight paleness and quivering of the lip." In other words, the prince recognized Williams as the "lost dauphin," Louis XVII, the heir to the throne, now grown into adulthood.

According to Williams, the prince informed him (in private, of course) that Williams was the heir to the throne and produced a document asking him to relinquish the title in exchange for certain titles and payments, but Williams declined to sign the document; he would rather live anonymously in poverty and exile than "barter away the rights pertaining to him by his birth." What an honorable guy.

In the United States, the legend told of royalist sympathizers saving the boy-prince from the bloody revolution by smuggling him away to colonial America to be raised by an Indian couple.

Williams, who was raised by Indians but hated to admit it, a man who made an avocation of fantasizing about his royal heritage, staked his claim to be Louis XVII. He would act out when seeing books about the French Revolution, focusing on the portrait of the young prince's prison tormentor, shaking uncontrollably and crying, "That image has haunted me day and night, as long as I can remember. 'Tis the horrid vision of my dreams. What is it? Who is it?"

In 1851, Williams hit the jackpot. After a chance meeting with a reporter for *Putnam's Magazine*, the publication ran an article presenting Williams's claim to be the prince. It captured the public's imagination. *Putnam's* reportedly increased its readership by twenty thousand people. The story was adapted into a book, *The Lost Prince*.

Over and over Williams would feign his trauma at seeing images of the French Revolution in books and periodicals:

> I got near enough without taking fright to see a book spread open on the blanket, showing two illuminated pages. Something parted in me. I saw my mother, as I had seen her in some past life . . . a fair oval-faced mother with arched brows. I saw even her pointed waist and puffed skirts, and the lace around her open neck. . . .
>
> I dropped on my knees and stretched my arms above my head, crying aloud as women cry with gasps and chokings in sudden bereavement. Nebulous memories twisted all around me and I could grasp nothing. I raged for what had been mine—for some high estate out of which I had fallen into degradation.

The "lost dauphin" became a celebrity. The *New York Times* reported, "Mr. Williams visited this City, and was received with great consideration; levees were held in his honor; his

MICHAEL BIE PHOTO

Lost Dauphin Park, De Pere, Wis.

portrait was in all the galleries; and for a time he was extensively
lionized."

Never mind that his own mother disavowed the story. She
was asked, along with two elderly members of the St. Regis tribe,
whether Eleazor was her own son or a child brought to her for
care. Each denounced the tale as a lie, his mother bursting into
tears and saying she knew Eleazor was two-faced but she didn't
know he was so bad as to deny his own mother.

Eleazor Williams died August 28, 1858, in Hogansburg,
New York, on the St. Regis Indian Reservation, the place of his
birth whether he admitted it or not. In his final years it seems he
became increasingly unglued and claimed assassins were after him.

Williams's tale of being the lost prince survived him in northeast Wisconsin with a mix of intrigue and bemusement. Lost Dauphin Road runs past the hillside on the Fox River where his home held sweeping vistas of the river. A historical marker reads in part: "In 1822 Williams led a delegation of New York Indians to the Fox River Valley, hoping to set up an Indian Empire in the West. . . . In 1841 the French Prince de Joinville visited Williams at Green Bay, giving rise to the belief he might be the 'Lost Dauphin,' son of Louis XVI and Marie Antoinette. This story gained wide publicity in 1853 through the book *The Lost Prince* by John H. Hanson. Williams had scars like those borne by little Louis XVII. Was he the Lost Dauphin?"

In 1947, a century after his death, his remains were relocated from New York to Oneida, Wisconsin. Anthropologists took the opportunity to study his bones and came to the conclusion he probably was of Indian descent. Still, there was no conclusive evidence.

At long last, the truth of the prince's fate was verified in 2000, and the true story of the evidence exceeds any tall tales fabricated by impostors in the American frontier.

The prince was imprisoned after the bloody revolution toppled his parents King Louis XVI and Queen Marie Antoinette. Held in squalid conditions for more than two years, the boy eventually succumbed to tuberculosis in 1795.

A doctor performed an autopsy the next day, and stole the boy's heart by slipping it into a handkerchief and dropping into his coat pocket. The organ was kept in a glass case on the doctor's bookshelf, preserved in alcohol, which evaporated over time. In 1810, the heart was stolen by one of the doctor's students. Later, as the student was dying of tuberculosis, he confessed to his wife, who returned the heart to the doctor who had stolen it the first time. He gave it to the archbishop of Paris.

Then yet another French Revolution arrived on the scene. In 1830 the archbishop's residence was stormed by angry mobs. A struggle ensued between a worker attempting to protect the heart and one of the revolutionaries. The crystal case containing the heart was shattered in the struggle. Days later the sympathetic worker found the organ amid shards of glass in a pile of sand in the courtyard. The heart survived and in 1975 was presented to the basilica of St. Denis to lie with other royal relics.

But the rumor of the boy's escape into exile—and that the organ belonged to some other nameless child—persisted across more than two centuries. Thanks to modern science, the answer came in 2000.

"The mystery finally ended today: DNA analysis confirmed that the heart of the young king rests in a crystal globe in a basilica in a suburb of Paris," reported news services. "Experts said that the evidence provided by the telltale heart offers scientific proof that Louis-Charles, the son of King Louis XVI and Queen Marie Antoinette, both guillotined during the French Revolution, died shortly thereafter at the age of 10, ending a theoretical two-year reign as Louis XVII.

The heart that reposes at the basilica in St. Denis with other royal remains and relics has always been said to be that of the young king, who died of tuberculosis two years after the execution of his parents at what is now the Place de la Concorde, at the southern end of the Champs Elysees. But there has never been any proof. Over the years, one pretender after another has sprung up to claim that Louis XVII—he technically became king following the death of his father in 1793—was spirited away alive and a body of another child left in his place.

Williams died in a small cabin built to resemble a French chateau. Before his death a visitor reported, "His household presented an aspect of cheerless desolation, without a mitigating ray of comfort, or a genial spark of homelight." Hanging on a peg on the wall was a silk dress, a gown once worn by his mother, the Queen Marie Antoinette, he told visitors.

Wrote one historian: "Out of this world he had ridden away in a delusion of regal ancestral lineage."

"It's called 'living off your story,'" said Ann Koski, former director of Green Bay's public museum. "People like that get invited to parties, to weeklong retreats, basically by the rich who wanted to have interesting guests. You don't need to have visible means of support; you live off your story, and he did that for a long time."

CHAPTER 4

A Capitol Offense

Byron Kilbourn sat down at the desk in his house on the corner of Grand Avenue and Fourth Street in Milwaukee, and putting quill to parchment, began to make lists, as powerful men are known to do. It was the fall of 1856. An enormous land grant had been awarded by the state legislature to the La Crosse & Milwaukee Railroad Company to build a line spanning Wisconsin. As president of the company, Kilbourn had thank-you notes to deliver, a normally mundane task, but in this instance delivering the notes required innovation, foresight, planning, execution . . . and a lot of subterfuge. Kilbourn was up to the task.

On one page he listed the names of each state-elected official opposite a number. On the second page he carried over the numbers and set them opposite another figure—five, ten, fifteen, etc. The two pages worked as a virtual lock and key; one was useless without the other. The number representing the official from the first page was written on the outside of an envelope.

Portrait of Byron Kilbourn (Whi-62389).

The corresponding number from the second page—five, ten, fifteen, etc.—represented railroad company stocks and bonds in increments of thousands; those, of course, were for the insides of the envelopes.

Kilbourn delegated, as powerful men are known to do, the rest of the task to the railroad company's comptroller, who needed no further explanation. When the comptroller saw the largest figure on the second page, sixty, representing sixty thousand dollars worth of bonds, he turned to Kilbourn and grinned.

"That must be Governor Bashford."

Indeed.

By the end of the day, the comptroller had divvied up more than a half-million dollars in bonds, all neatly counted and placed in envelopes addressed with a simple number on the outside.

Byron Kilbourn was a big man. Tall and commanding, he looked contemporaries in the eyes when speaking, using his considerable reputation to impose his will whenever necessary. A civil engineer by training, Kilbourn helped establish Milwaukee as we know it and then served as mayor of the city he created. He was a legislator, one of the authors of the Wisconsin state constitution, and a candidate for US Senate. When Kilbourn was not occupied with public policy he was the driving force in a number of business enterprises, not the least of which was developing railroad lines in Wisconsin. It was said Kilbourn possessed "will of iron, good judgment, excellent executive abilities, great brain power, saw far away into the future, and possessed a magnetism that would both attract and attach to himself and his plans to all who came under his influence . . . a born leader."

In early Wisconsin, the manner in which a born leader got things done was distinctly different than today.

At stake in 1856 was the prize of prizes: 546,000 acres of land bestowed by the federal government for the purpose of building a railroad line from the Madison area to Superior. Kilbourn had been the principal organizer of the first Wisconsin railroad line built between Milwaukee and Waukesha, and he served as the company president until 1852 when he was forced to resign because of alleged fraud and mismanagement.

Kilbourn's latest endeavor, created to snare the immense bounty of the 1856 land grant, was the La Crosse & Milwaukee Railroad. The group competing against him for the land grant was the Milwaukee & Mississippi Railroad, Kilbourn's former company.

The land would be awarded to one of the two companies by approval of the state legislature.

First Kilbourn needed a man who knew his way around the brutish politics of Madison. This was the place where, a decade earlier, an argument that broke out on the floor of the legislative chamber resulted in the shooting death of a Green Bay assemblyman. And corruption was laid bare in the gubernatorial election of 1855 when Democrat incumbent William Barstow was declared the winner by 157 votes. It was discovered that Barstow's win was due to forged election returns coming from nonexistent precincts in northern Wisconsin. With rival militia units converging on the state capital, Republican Coles Bashford was sworn in quietly on January 7, 1856, while Barstow was publicly inaugurated with full pomp and circumstance. Wisconsin had two governors. The state attorney general acted to remove Barstow, who threatened that he would not give up his office alive. But Barstow did give up alive when the tide of public opinion turned against him, and he handed the governor's office to Lieutenant Governor Arthur MacArthur. The next day, with a court order and a throng of well-armed followers in tow, Bashford entered the capitol and evicted MacArthur.

Historian Fred Holmes summed up Wisconsin's political landscape this way:

> Few western states can offer a more turbulent official record than that in Wisconsin in the twenty years that preceded the Civil War. Pioneer civilizations always seemed to be tinged with greed and fanaticism. During these years in Wisconsin the political atmosphere was white-hot with partisanship; officials 'feathered their nests' at public expense; the vast land heritage of the estate was wantonly squandered and public morals touched bottom. It was an epoch fogged with political trickery and legislative chicanery.

Against this backdrop of wide-open frontier politics, the fate of the massive land grant rested in the grubby hands of state legislators.

Byron Kilbourn, representing the railroad, found his right-hand man in a longtime ally, the bold and brash Moses Strong, who like Kilbourn had a seemingly flexible conscience.

Strong's reputation as an ambitious and colorful figure in early Wisconsin preceded him. The Mineral Point lawyer was best known for drinking "long and frequently" from pitchers of whiskey, and he had narrowly escaped public disgrace years earlier for mismanagement of territorial funds. Strong had the energy and the connections to become governor. The problem was that even his fellow Democrats loathed him. He held a number of important positions in the territory and early statehood; out of office by the mid 1850s, the "Knight of the Pitcher" was running a modestly successful law office and speculating in losing business ventures.

Kilbourn placed Strong on the La Crosse & Milwaukee payroll as legal counsel, then arranged for Strong to be elected to a Milwaukee assembly district, despite the latter's residency in Mineral Point.

So it was business as usual in 1856 for two founding fathers of Wisconsin. The men went to work, Kilbourn lobbying politicians from the outside, Strong working the inside. Their efforts resulted in the land grant being awarded overwhelmingly to the La Crosse & Milwaukee Railroad, Byron Kilbourn, president, Moses Strong, legal counsel.

After the grant's approval in October 1856, Kilbourn— the "born leader" who possessed "excellent executive abilities" and "great brain power"—devised the ingenious method of distributing payments to officials. The second page of his lock and key, the page containing only numbers, was needed by the company for accounting purposes. The first page, containing the list of public officials and their designated number, was used by Kilbourn and Strong to deliver the envelopes to the correct recipients. Kilbourn tossed the first list into the nearest fireplace once the bonds were delivered.

Kilbourn himself was rewarded handsomely by the La Crosse & Milwaukee Railroad for his part in securing the grant. True to form, the savvy Kilbourn knew better than to receive his cut in unrealized bonds. Parcels of prime real estate valued at thirty thousand dollars (somewhere north of seven hundred thousand in today's dollars) were included in his compensation.

For two years rumors of corruption clouded the state capitol. Newly elected Governor Alexander Randall's first message to the legislature of 1858 established an investigating committee to look into the matter. It was raining subpoenas in no time.

"Did you promise or give any member of the Legislature of 1856 to understand," the committee asked Kilbourn, "that he should be in any way rewarded or compensated for his vote?"

"This interrogatory is so general in terms, and wide in its scope," Kilbourn started, "that I deem the most appropriate mode of answering it will be to give a connected statement of all the transactions in which I was concerned as an agent of the La Crosse & Milwaukee Railroad Company."

An hour later he was still talking—and still had not answered the question. Finally, two thirds of the way through his impressive, if not tedious, recitation of all his dealings with the company, Kilbourn began to address the payoffs.

"To the best of my recollection . . . I never offered, nor agreed, nor promised, to or with any member of the legislature" payments for awarding the land grant. "Nor did I know any other person making such offer, promise or agreement; and further, that I have never paid to any such member, any bond, stock or other thing, in consideration of any vote so given, nor do I know of any other person having made any such payment; nor do I know of any member of the legislature having received any such payment."

His "constant effort," Kilbourn droned on, was to impress upon the legislature by all lawful means "the importance of securing the benefits that would flow to Wisconsin, from possession of this grant, by a company within our own state."

In the same breath Kilbourn continued, "I caused it to be understood . . . that in the event of the La Crosse company obtaining the grant, that company would acknowledge the favor by a liberal gratuity to such members as should favor its passage."

The big man was dancing on thin ice. No payments were made in exchange for votes, he was testifying, but gratuities— just innocent little thank-you gifts—were promised and given to those who voted in favor of the company. Even Kilbourn seemed to hold his nose on that point. "Whether such an argument would bear the strictest test of morality, was not for me to determine." He was just doing what he was told by the company's board of directors in the name of "state pride, as a measure for the protection of state interests, which was doubtless all right."

By the way, Kilbourn added, many of the legislators told him a payoff "would be expected, and indeed was necessary to success."

Kilbourn never did explain why the elaborate shell game was necessary to conceal the recipients' identities if the payments were harmless "gratuities."

The rough-edged Moses Strong was far less diplomatic than his partner in gratuities. First he refused to testify and had to be jailed for six days, arguing that legislative committees do not have subpoena powers. (The case went to the state Supreme Court, where his argument was rejected.) He spoke eventually, making it clear he thought the gratuity business was sordid stuff even by his own whiskey-soaked standards.

"It has been the habit of my life to make and preserve written memoranda of all events or circumstances that I desire to remember," Strong said. "I had no desire to remember anything about the delivery of those packages. My office for a day or two was thronged with members of the Legislature and others, who, I suppose, came there to receive the packages. I got rid of them as soon as possible."

The final report was published May 13, 1858. Five thousand copies were printed, and nearly all were seized and burned by implicated politicians. There are two copies in the archives of the state historical society; the legislative reference bureau was never able to secure a copy. Despite the hijinks involving the printed copies, the results made their way to newspapers, and a wave of outrage swept Madison from across the state and nation.

"The evidence taken," the report states, "establishes the fact that the managers of the La Crosse & Milwaukee Railroad

Company have been guilty of numerous and unparalleled acts of mismanagement, gross violations in duty, fraud and plunder. In fact, corruption and wholesale plundering are common features."

The report implicated thirteen state senators, fifty-nine members of the assembly, the state bank comptroller, the lieutenant governor, the private secretary of the governor, three officers of the assembly, twenty-three lobbyists, and a justice of the state supreme court. All told, more than six hundred thousand dollars in construction bonds (which were being derided as "corruption bonds"), as well as stocks and cash, were delivered.

The investigation doomed the La Crosse & Milwaukee Railroad Company. The bonds slipped into eager legislative hands were rendered worthless with the company's liquidation.

Nobody was ever prosecuted. It was deemed the payoffs were unsought, that nothing of value exchanged hands to obtain votes. Kilbourn's scheme of promising a generous gratuity, a mere thank-you gift after the vote, saved the hide of many a greedy pol.

Less than two years later the nation plunged into civil war and the wholesale corruption of the Wisconsin state government faded into obscurity.

History is mixed on the fate of the participants. Governor Coles Bashford—the only person to cash in his bonds before the railroad company folded—left office in 1858 and departed the state just as the investigation was heating up. He ended up in the Arizona Territory and was appointed its first attorney general. He served in a number of prominent positions in the territory (as an independent, rather than with his former Republican Party) and ran a general store in Prescott until his death in 1878. Today the Republican Party of Wisconsin annually bestows the Coles Bashford Award to the organization's top volunteer.

Moses Strong, the Knight of the Pitcher, "despite his optimism, ambition and native intelligence, never achieved the political power and monetary fortune which he sought," according to the Wisconsin Historical Society. Prone to shortcuts, gambling, and heavy drinking, Strong saw his business and political fortunes plummet following the economic collapse of 1857 and the corruption investigation the following year. Strong returned to his Mineral Point law practice and served as president of the state bar association from 1878 to1893. From 1871 until his death he was vice president of the Wisconsin Historical Society.

Byron Kilbourn's career was "ruined" by the scandal, according to his biography with the Wisconsin Historical Society. In 1858, perhaps in a move to recover his reputation, he attempted to start a liberal arts college named Kilbourn University (modesty never was his strong suit) for poor boys. The legislature denied his request for a charter and he retired from public life. He is commonly remembered today as one of the founders of Milwaukee with Solomon Juneau and George Walker. Historic Milwaukee, Inc., maintains Kilbourn remained a "respected and powerful citizen." The book *History of Milwaukee: City and County,* written in 1922, devotes considerable copy to Kilbourn, as it should, yet never mentions the scandal, describing him as "sociable, communicative, benevolent and always ready to engage in anything to help his adopted city." He moved to Florida in 1868 for health reasons and died two years later. In 1998 Historic Milwaukee, Inc., arranged to have the big man's remains, ensconced in a twelve hundred-pound cast-iron casket, returned to Milwaukee and interned in Forest Home Cemetery.

Amasa Cobb, an assemblyman from Iowa County, was one of the few men who told Kilbourn and Strong what they could do with their money. He was known ever after as Honest Amasa Cobb. He served with distinction as a congressman representing southwest Wisconsin and has a village named after him in Iowa County.

CHAPTER 5

"A Horrid Dread": The Unsolved Murder of H. C. Mead

Henry Mead did not show up for dinner.

As peculiar as Mr. Mead was—refusing to consume hot food until it went cold, for example—he nevertheless ate every meal at the boardinghouse located one block from his business, the Exchange Bank of Waupaca, before taking his evening stroll and returning to work.

Having no family in Waupaca, Mead usually stayed around the clock inside the tiny bank and slept on a cot in the back room. The bank was reliable, unlike many others of the day; its founder had a miserly reputation (using pencils until they were worn to the nub) even though he was a soft touch when it came to charity.

So when the somewhat odd but always dependable "H. C." Mead failed to show up for Sunday dinner on October 8, 1882, two boardinghouse waitresses walked over to his simple white bank building.

One of the girls rapped on the front door. Hearing nothing, she cupped her hands around her eyes and peered through the front window. The other walked around to the office in back. She found a large wooden box against the building and boosted herself to the open window above.

"I can't see in," she said to her companion.

"Push the curtain over."

"I don't think I ought to."

Not wanting to pry but concerned for the old man, she reluctantly brushed the curtain aside with the back of her hand.

"The scene which presented itself on looking into the window was of the most sickening character," reported a local newspaper. Mead's body was on the floor next to his desk, "the room was spattered with blood, the floor smeared with gore, and pools of blood had collected against the baseboard."

Other accounts described "great chunks of oozing flesh" driven into the wall by a shotgun blast. "Both of his eyes, most of his nose, and that part of his face from the cheek bone to the left eye had been shot away, and flesh and blood were lying on the floor several feet from the corpse." Bloody handprints stained the walls.

The girls' screams alerted residents. Within moments a crowd gathered around the building. While the scene was gruesome, most folks whispered it wasn't surprising. Every night the tall old banker with the long gray beard took a walk through the downtown before returning to work, where he opened the safe and worked alone into the early hours. Everyone in Waupaca

Mead Bank today, Waupaca, Wis.

knew Mead and his routine. Even in reporting his brutal death, one local newspaper noted the banker's unconventional work habits and asked, "Could anything be more careless?" The *Waupaca Post* coldly promoted its extra edition with the headline: "H. C. Meade, the Banker, Cashes His Last Check."

A month following the murder, reported by newspapers across the country, the county sheriff announced all attempts to find the culprit had been exhausted. Residents felt otherwise. The unsettling feeling that a number of perpetrators were living free in Waupaca clouded the community. The *Waupaca Republican* pointed to a "long list of crimes committed here during the past four or five years" and declared, "We do not remember but one case where the guilty party has been detected and punished.

Besides this we have had an unchecked reign of rowdyism, ruffianism, drunkenness, gambling, debauchery, licentiousness, and all those vices that tend to demoralize a community and destroy law and order."

In January 1883, three months after Mead's death, three drifters were arrested following a tip from a "girl of choice habits" in Stevens Point. In the days coinciding with the murder the three suspects had whiled away their time in Point's "low saloons and houses of ill-fame." They disappeared the day of the murder and returned the next day with rolls of cash, most definitely not their usual financial state of affairs.

But the case unraveled in no time. The drifters had solid alibis to their whereabouts. The Stevens Point prostitute turned out to be the estranged wife of lead suspect Alfred Vandecar. More interestingly, it was revealed that a bag of bonds, loans, and other notes from the bank robbery had been dumped in a Waupaca alley days after the murder.

"The only theory is that someone living in Waupaca threw the papers there," the newspaper wrote, "and hundreds of people in Waupaca believe that a Waupaca man had a hand in it or was privy to the business" of robbing and shooting Mead.

It was also determined that the wadding used in the shotgun—found scattered across the crime scene—was newsprint from the *Waupaca Post*.

The lead suspect among the three drifters remained in jail for a year as the prosecution vainly searched for more evidence.

"The people are beginning to talk about the pursuit of and arrest of Vandecar as a grand piece of swindling with the intent to bleed the county of large sums of money" for expenses, reported one newspaper. The *Weyauwega Chronicle* was more explicit, calling the detectives, policemen, and district attorney "leeches."

"The people of this county must have a large stock of patience or are a set of numbskulls to let this go on and not raise a voice against the 'ring' that encircles the courthouse," reported the *Chronicle.*

The Vandecar trial occurred early in 1884. After forty-four hours of deliberation the jury was hung up with neither side budging. The defendant was free to go.

Six years passed. The unsolved murder of banker Mead festered all the while. In November 1890 the Waupaca county board offered a two thousand-dollar reward for the apprehension and conviction of Mead's killer. Immediately following the approval of the reward, officials arrested Charles "Tab" Prior, a former Waupaca police officer.

"All sorts of rumors are afloat as to the probable outcome of the matter, and public opinion is split about evenly as to whether there will be a conviction," the newspaper wrote. "Names of prominent businessmen are connected to the affair."

But no new evidence was introduced with Prior's arrest, and the district attorney declined to prosecute following an inquest.

"A fearful strain, and sort of a horrid dread seemed to hang like a cloud" over Waupaca, reported the *Oshkosh Northwestern.*

"It was oppressive and unreal. The freedom of the people was chilled and the ghost of secrecy seemed stalking abroad by day and night. The feeling was general that the perpetrators were daily mingling with the citizens; that a small conclave of those within the secret was ready to adopt any means in their desperation to throttle the discovery of the guilty parties."

Waupaca was at odds with itself. Accusations and rumor-mongering were still rampant a decade after the murder. A former Waupaca newspaper editor publicly accused Fred Lea, a longtime businessman, former mayor, and the state representative, of committing the crime. Lea responded with a slander suit. The civic tension finally sparked a serious examination of the crime with the creation of a grand jury in March 1892.

After a month of diligent work the grand jury handed down indictments of three men for the murder and five more as accessories. All were residents of Waupaca at the time of the crime; some were members of Waupaca's pioneer families. The three primary suspects were Sam Stout, owner of the tavern located near Mead's bank, which served as a popular watering hole for the hard-drinking local political establishment; Tab Prior, the former night watchman who had been arrested and released two years earlier; and Ed Bronson, a local merchant who had been financed by Mead. Among the five men named as accessories to be tried at a later date was Fred Lea, the former mayor who was serving in the Wisconsin legislature at the time of the indictments.

"Waupaca has furnished numerous sensations in times past, but few of them have eclipsed the latest commotion occasioned by the indictments found by the grand jury against several citizens of the place," the newspaper reported.

The Waupaca County district attorney hired Joseph Very Quarles for the prosecution. Quarles was a distinguished attorney from Milwaukee, decorated Civil War veteran, and elected official who would go on to serve in the United States Senate.

"The trial of the case will be the greatest ever known in Wisconsin there is no doubt," wrote the *Milwaukee Sentinel.* "The legal talent on both sides is among the best known lawyers in the state. "

Quarles alluded to the unique challenges facing the prosecution.

"There is not so much mystery in the case itself, as in that unseen, powerful influence which has for so many closed the eyes of the officers and sealed the lips of the people who should be witnesses in this case. There is mystery in that."

Prosecutors believed they needed a certain piece of evidence to help present their case. On a winter day months before the trial, three men trudged to Mead's final resting place with shovels in hand, dreading their chore—and not just because the ground was frozen. Their labors resulted in a stunned courtroom as prosecutors held aloft the exhumed skull of Henry Mead, the frontal lobe blown clean off from the shotgun blast.

"On the night of October 7, 1882," Quarles began, "the old man took his usual stroll. He was a gossip, he was a meddler.

He meddled with the young men who reveled nights and rode with strange women. One of those men was in business. He had threatened this man and we will show you that he had told him that he would withdraw his aid."

Quarles explained that Bronson had loans coming due, and the merchant and the banker were seen in a heated discussion the day of the murder. Later that day Bronson met Tab Prior in a Waupaca barber shop. The two men had a whispered conversation and borrowed the barber's shotgun. Prior had incurred Mead's wrath for associating with the clique of young turks who were dominating Waupaca. Bronson was seen standing on the street corner near the bank just before the murder. Quarles believed Bronson served as the lookout, while Prior and Sam Stout did the dirty work.

Another grand jury witness identified Prior and Stout as the two men who visited a livery stable about midnight. The two men changed their clothes and washed up, telling the livery hand not to say a word—they had been with some "sporting" women. When their blood-stained clothes were discovered later, Stout warned the stable hand to keep quiet about it.

The final link in Quarles's case came from William Hanscomb, who told prosecutors he helped Prior leave town immediately after the murder, contradicting Prior's alibi.

Day after day in ninety-degree temperatures throughout the summer of 1892 the packed courtroom heard the lawyers match wits. "This will be a long trial and a trial that will depend largely on circumstantial evidence," Quarles told the jury; it would be up to them to "put together the circumstances tending to show the guilt of the defendants."

The defense team exploited the circumstantial evidence at every turn. Making matters more difficult for Quarles were witnesses who became less sure of themselves in the courtroom than they were during the grand jury inquest. The biggest blow occurred when William Hanscomb, while on the stand, denied everything he had told prosecutors prior to the trial. Allegations of payoffs flew. Hanscomb was arrested for perjury.

The trial dragged on for six weeks. The jury dragged on far less. The three men were acquitted after twenty-four minutes of deliberation. Having only circumstantial evidence and unreliable witnesses, Quarles could not prove beyond reasonable doubt the men were inside the bank that night, even though it was believed the guilty parties were among the group indicted. The second trial for the accessories was dropped. (Hanscomb was convicted of perjury and sent to prison.)

The Mead matter was closed, legally speaking. At the same time it settled nothing other than ensuring the perpetrators never would face justice. No further official efforts were made to solve the mystery. Mead's skull was placed in a box along with the other evidence and left in the courthouse.

The case gathered public notoriety one last time, in 1929, when the *Milwaukee Journal* reportedly "solved" the crime. The newspaper's story, based on information provided by an anonymous "old timer," reported that one of the three accused men from the trial made a deathbed confession.

Sheriff E. J. Flanagan, deceased, obtained a full confession in 1907. One of the three men acquitted of the murder was a hard drinker. He became ill and told the whole story to the sheriff. Another confession was obtained from the daughter of one of the other men, corroborating the first. Before action was taken the confessed slayer died. Sheriff Flanagan was informed that this left him with small chance of convicting the other six and by advice did not obtain warrants.

The article never states it, but the alleged deathbed confessor would have been Sam Stout, who continued to operate his Waupaca tavern until his death in 1907. Tab Prior had died in 1894. Bronson had moved away.

While the perpetrators are shrouded in a mystery, their actions are not. . . .

Following a raucous political meeting rife with drinking and grandstanding the night of October 7, 1882, the clique of hard-charging young men gathered at Stout's saloon to continue the revelry. Knowing the pious Mead was taking his evening walk, one or more of the group snuck down the alley behind the bank, cut through the screen in the back window, and hid in a closet. Others took lookout positions. Predictably Mead returned to the bank and began working at his desk. The man or men sprang from the closet and clubbed the banker from behind, inflicting deep cuts on the back of his head. Dazed and bleeding profusely, Mead groped his way around the office, leaving his bloody handprints on the walls before staggering back to his chair and collapsing at his desk. The men grabbed some cash and bonds; they left more than they took. Perhaps their intent was stealing the banker's bundle of loans with the drunken idea that the debtors among them could destroy the paperwork.

One thing didn't go as planned, though. At some point— either when he was reeling from being struck on the head, or after regaining consciousness at his desk—Mead caught a glimpse of the perpetrators.

Then, as Quarles stated during the trial, "A professional burglar, having his plunder, would have escaped, he would have no reason to murder, but if the men who robbed the bank lived right here, a second crime was necessary. As sure as night follows day, a man who commits a crime has got to commit another to cover it up. Those men, filled with liquor, finished Mead off."

The identity of those men and the role each played remains a secret for the ages.

It was said that the "unchecked reign" of lawlessness that had plagued Waupaca at the time of Mead's death ended that night. "After this terrible crime all drunkenness and carousing ceased and never has been resumed," according to an 1893 newspaper account, which noted that one of the indicted men, Fred

Grave marker of Henry C. Mead.

Lea, "was pretty wild up to the time of the murder, but since then he has been straight as a string."

Succeeding generations of Waupaca residents would tell the story about the banker's murder on a dark and stormy night. His name was whispered during backyard campouts when the evening produced strange sounds. Schoolchildren learning about local history made the rite-of-passage field trip to view the grisly evidence stored in the courthouse.

It was 1990, more than a century after the murder, when a local funeral home director lobbied officials to return Mead's remains to his, well, remains. A judge agreed the skull no longer served any evidentiary purpose. It was removed from the courthouse, cremated, and placed in Lakeside Memorial Cemetery where H. C. Mead today rests in peace, hopefully.

But it's doubtful whether anyone who knows the story can rest comfortably knowing that justice was never served, that inside the old Exchange Bank of Waupaca, the "Mead Bank," hidden underneath decades of paint and dust, exists the mark of Cain left by the perpetrators on that stormy evening, crimson stains made indelible as only the blood of the innocent can be.

CHAPTER 6

"Plaster John": The Miracle Healer of Somerset

Octave Cloutier could see John Till was no typical doctor. Unshaven, with yellow, tobacco-stained teeth, Till's clothes were filthy. He went without shoes, his feet looking as though they had never been washed. His ears were pierced with gold earrings. Nevertheless Cloutier explained to Till the dire condition of his wife and the two men departed immediately for Somerset, Till taking nothing with him but a bucket containing a strange oil, which smelled a lot like kerosene.

It was the fall of 1905. Meline Cloutier was suffering from an increasingly serious infection in her cheek. Despite attention from the doctor in Somerset, Mrs. Cloutier's condition had become grave. Her husband, desperate to save his wife, was told that a man named John Till in Almena had performed healings.

Till applied his ointment to Mrs. Cloutier's open sore, explaining that his treatment would draw the infection out of her body. It wasn't pleasant. The concoction in his bucket caused the skin to blister badly. The prescription, Till explained, was taught to him in his homeland of Austria. Diseases and "all other ailments," he explained in his thick Austrian accent, everything from cancer to bunions, were caused by poisons in the body. Draw the poisons out and the body is healed, he said. The oozing blisters caused by the burning ointment would do just that.

And soon after, Mrs. Cloutier's infection went away.

Somerset was abuzz with the news. The Cloutiers, true believers in Till's cure, began recruiting neighbors and residents to seek treatment from the backwoodsman. In no time, Till was traveling to Somerset on a regular basis to apply his miracle ointment to folks lined up in Cloutier's farmhouse.

Word continued to spread of the miracle healer. Business boomed so much that Till moved into to the Cloutier's home and Octave began serving as his manager.

Wagon after wagon, as many as thirty rigs a day, transported patients to the Cloutier home from the Somerset depot. Residents did a booming business providing transportation, rooms, and board for visitors. Saloons were brimming with visitors. Cloutier added a treatment room to his home.

From 6 a.m. until 10 p.m., Till and Cloutier sat six patients at a time on backless chairs in the "clinic." According to one resident, "Till would feel the patient's jugular vein and tell them what their problem was. The sufferer's back was laid bare. Till would take his sponge and smear his concoction from neck to base of spine. Cloutier in the meantime would sew in the person's

Photo of John Till taken in New Richmond, Wis.

garments some cotton batting. This would soak up the running matter from the skin inflamed by Till's powerful counter-irritant. In time the back would almost be like raw beef. The batting would remain two weeks and then a second treatment might be in store."

Till never asked for payment. Patients "each contributed as much as he deemed fit" wrote a reporter, "none less than a dollar, which sums were carelessly thrown into the treasury box to the rear of the thrifty and industrious operator who appeared not to give it a thought."

One silver dollar was the typical gratuity. Live chickens were another. Till deposited as much as three thousand dollars every two weeks over a four-year period—all carried to the bank in five-gallon buckets. Cloutier received fifty cents on every dollar.

Somerset was a "whirl of excitement," reported the *Stillwater Messenger*.

"Hotels in Stillwater and Hudson were booked solid, and bars at Somerset grossed as much as one hundred dollars a day at a time when beer cost a nickel and whisky was fifteen cents a shot," according to the *Wisconsin Magazine of History*. "One farmer, making the best of the housing shortage, spread clean hay on the floors of his two-story barn and did a 'thriving business' charging thirty-five cents for sleeping accommodations, bed clothing not furnished. Hotels, restaurants, saloons, and livery stables raked in large profits, thanks to the plaster doctor."

Till had become a celebrity. A folk song penned in 1907 started like this:

We took a trip to Somerset not very long ago,

On the borders of Wisconsin where the Apple River flows.

Our health it was so poorly that we thought that we would try

That Doctor there at Somerset, for he was all the cry.

A steady stream of reporters made their way to the Cloutier farm to observe the phenomenon of "Plaster John." One asked if he could watch the treatments.

"For vot purpose?" Till replied. "You have nottings de matter mit you."

"Nothing but a severe attack of curiosity," the reporter said.

"I'm too busy to help you satisfy dat!"

When asked about his rugged appearance, Till would say, "Remember, Christ who owns the whole world was dressed poorly."

With as many as 150 people a day receiving treatment and word traveling as far away as Canada, authorities inevitably began casting a skeptical eye on the plaster doctor of Somerset. The State Medical Board began hounding Till for practicing medicine without a license. When a man who was likely dead on arrival was deposited in the treatment room against Mrs. Cloutier's protests, the authorities were called and Till was charged in the man's death. He would be acquitted, but it was the start of years of arrests and court trials for Till. Still, juries of his peers could not be persuaded to convict Plaster John, and after each of his trials Till would be welcomed by brass bands and crowds of people eagerly awaiting treatment. As many as thirteen hundred patients were waiting for him following one court case in 1907.

"In the long run," the Hudson newspaper wrote, "Till is liable to have many more friends than the . . . [medical] board which is frantically determined to ding away at the legislature until they have made it a felony to take a dose of catnip tea or onion syrup without their prescription."

Till was born in Austria in 1870. As a boy he was involved in an accident with a hay wagon that broke both of his legs and fractured a number of ribs. Unable to afford a traditional doctor, his father had Till treated by a "healing blacksmith." The boy had a deformed leg as a result of the accident. The treatment made an impression on the young Till and he spent his formative years learning folk treatments from the blacksmith and a monk. He emigrated to Wisconsin in 1898 to work as a lumberjack.

Initially Till called his miracle ointment "4X." It was a blend of kerosene and croton oil, a "poisonous viscous liquid obtained from the seeds of a small Asiatic tree." He modified the recipe and the treatment to deal with the large numbers of people seeking help in Somerset. The plaster-like substance was administered in one of three doses: mild, strong, and for life-threatening illnesses, "horse treatment." The mixture was sponged on the back, which immediately began to boil and blister, supposedly lifting the toxins out of the patient's body.

In 1908, he and the Cloutiers visited Till's birthplace in Austria. On their return to the states Till was delayed at Ellis Island because of his crippled leg. Apparently the Cloutiers decided to return to Somerset while Till was detained. Feeling slighted, Till never returned to Somerset, ending the lucrative three-year partnership with Octave Cloutier and sending Somerset into an economic freefall. Despite the desperate pleadings of Somerset, Till chose to set up shop with his sister back in Almena.

Business in Almena picked up right where it left off. The miracle healer built a two-story clinic called the House of John Till. As in Somerset, the economic impact on his community was Till's greatest ally. In 1909 as many as six hundred people a week were visiting the house. "One night," the *Cumberland Advocate* reported, "20 [people] had to sit in chairs in the Hotel Mason and over 50 slept in the depot."

Till's carefree and unsophisticated management of a booming business marked the beginning of the end. After his split with Octave Cloutier he became an easy mark for everyone, from relatives to business partners and hucksters. He had a falling out with his sister, who established her own practice, and eventually Till fell prey to bad investments, lawsuits, swindlers, and—as always—the medical board.

As Till moved from Somerset to Almena to Turtle Lake and other places throughout northwest Wisconsin from 1909 to 1920, the medical board followed with arrest warrants for practicing medicine without a license. The press coverage became more critical: "There have been so many cases of horrible suffering occasioned by visits to Till that we are ashamed to chronicle them," said the *Stillwater Daily Gazette*. Till never called himself a doctor or charged for his treatment, points that saved him in previous court cases, but in 1920 his luck ran out. In Barron he was found guilty of practicing medicine without a license and sentenced to six months in jail. A petition signed by 6,500 people—including five doctors—was presented to the court, and the miracle healer was released on one condition. "Till has promised to leave the country," reported the *Hudson Star Observer*, "which is something we can all be grateful for."

He returned to a sizable property in Dittersdorf, Austria, in 1922. Reportedly he lost everything to the Nazis during World War II and returned to the United States penniless. John Till died of a heart attack while visiting friends in Kiel, Wisconsin, on July 14, 1947.

"What were the reasons for John Till's popularity?" asked a biographer, James Taylor Dunn, in 1956. "Why did so many thousands storm his door demanding the magic plaster and salve? Why do stories of miraculous cures affected by this wonder healer still circulate in the St. Croix Valley?"

The Chippewa Valley Museum echoes similar questions: "Was Till the 'wonder healer' many claimed he was or simply a charlatan? Certainly, there seems to have been no science behind his medicine. And although he never charged a penny, he reaped aplenty. Still many folks—it seems—were glowing in their testimonials. Chances are that Till meant only good, and perhaps he, like his thousands of followers, was a true believer."

The *Stillwater Messenger* offered an explanation during a Till trial in 1912: "He benefitted the health of thousands . . . whether or not there was anything supernatural in this or not, we do not presume to say. Whether people simply imagine Till has cured them, it is still a fact that a great many people claim Till cured them."

"Perhaps the explanation lies in the relative isolation of the farming community and its lack of competent medical assistance," Dunn wrote. "In their overwhelming desire for freedom from pain, these people were easy prey for all quacks and charlatans who made their fortunes from patent medicine and cure-all nostrums. Dr. Justus Ohage, as former St. Paul health commissioner, testified at one of Till's 1912 trials. He gave perhaps the best explanation: 'If a man suffering from stomach trouble applied to Till for treatment, he became absorbed in the condition of his blistered back and so forgot, by simple psychological process, all about his stomach distur-bance. There is just where the success of this man Till lies. When people go over there, as so many thousands do, they can't be fools! Some of the people are suffering from stomach trouble and when Till afflicts them and gives them sore backs, they can't think of anything else for months. They are so happy when their backs are healed that they do not think of their stomach troubles.'"

So off we start for Somerset, our hearts began to cheer,
We are all bound to reach the goal, for life it is so dear;
We know he's cured thousands, more feeble yet than we,
So all hurrah for Somerset, that Dr. there to see . . .

I can run and jump so nimble now, like 20 years ago,
So I thank the Doc at Somerset, and to him you all should go.

CHAPTER 7

The Life and Crimes of Pirate Captain Dan Seavey

Dan Seavey stepped ashore on the docks at Grand Haven, Michigan, armed with two of the most dangerous weapons known to man: booze and bad intentions.

It was the night of June 11, 1908, and by daybreak "Roaring Dan" was sailing into maritime history as the pirate of the Great Lakes.

Stealing a forty-ton ship and doing battle with a federal cutter will earn you that reputation.

Like all Great Lake ports, Grand Haven's harborside nightlife was ripe for a guy like Seavey, a sailor not above switching buoy lights to send ships aground so he could "salvage" the cargos after the crews departed. Nor was he opposed to running boatloads of poached deer, or using his ship as a floating whorehouse, or dropping a piano on an adversary's head.

With a fully stocked jug, Seavey easily befriended three marks that fateful June night in Grand Haven: the crew of the *Nellie Johnson*.

One thing about sharing a jug: You never know how much the other guy is drinking. Seavey allowed his companions to incapacitate themselves, likely faking his own swigs from the jug. With the crew literally under the table, Seavey commandeered the forty-ton *Nellie Johnson*, fully loaded with cargo, and set sail across Lake Michigan.

It took a day or so for the *Nellie Johnson*'s skipper to convince authorities he hadn't merely lost track of the ship in his drunken stupor.

Meanwhile, Seavey was shopping his ill-gotten booty in Chicago, where the big city harbor was teaming with folks who would buy his goods no questions asked. The harbormaster, however, had his suspicions. Maybe it was Seavey's assertion he had won the ship and its expensive cargo of cedar posts in a poker game. Perhaps it was Seavey's companion, a known counterfeiter with an outstanding arrest warrant in his name. Either way, Seavey ran up the *Nellie Johnson*'s sails and departed Chicago rather hastily. With that, the alarm went up and down the Lake Michigan shore: Dan Seavey had pirated the *Nellie Johnson*.

Piracy was a capital offense in 1908.

Captain Preston Ueberroth of the US Revenue Cutter Service in Milwaukee took the call, telling reporters, "I was asked to set out on a hunt for the man." With a federal marshal on board,

Ueberroth ordered the steamer *Tuscarora* loaded with coal and prepared for a chase.

A chase he got.

Sure, the facts and the fictions of Dan Seavey's life are so intermingled at this point in time that his exploits must be viewed with some degree of skepticism. Even his most widely reported adventure—the commandeering of the *Nellie Johnson*—contains widely conflicting accounts from the newspapers of the day. But scale down the tall tales and Seavey still looms large, particularly since the common threads of his life included monumental acts of drinking, brawling, whoring, poaching, and moon cussing.

Great Lakes historian Frederick Stonehouse profiled Seavey in the book *Great Lakes Crime* and provided the author with his bottom-line opinion: "Seavey was certainly a real low-life. Today he would be the guy stealing pop cans for the ten-cent deposit."

The mariners along the Atlantic seaboard knew all about "moon cussing," the nasty old pirate trick of rearranging or removing guide lights to send ships aground. When the crews abandoned ship, the pillaging commenced. It was in this no-holds-barred seafaring tradition that Dan Seavey learned the ropes. Born in Portland, Maine, in 1867, Seavey ran away at age thirteen to pursue the life of a tramp sailor.

"He arrived in northern Wisconsin near Marinette in the late 1880s, where he married a local girl with whom he had two daughters," according to an article published by the Wisconsin

Underwater Archeology Association (WUAA). "The family then moved to Milwaukee, where Dan fished, farmed and owned a local saloon near the waterfront."

Another old-time sailing tradition involves abandoning one's family. Seavey did just that when news of the Yukon gold rush reached the states in 1898. He was in his thirties when he returned to the Great Lakes region, penniless, about 1900. Seavey had already spent more than half his life living by his wits in the wildest ports-of-call in the world. With a schooner aptly named the *Wanderer*—obtained by means we can only imagine—Seavey was about to make the Inland Sea his personal playground.

"In reality the [cargo] business served as a cover for piracy," according to Tom Powers's book *Michigan Rogues, Desperadoes & Cutthroats.*

"Seavey and a small crew would silently slip the *Wanderer*, with no running lights, into ports in the dead of night and make off with anything on wharves, in unlocked warehouses, or on nearby streets that was of value and could be carried on the schooner."

To be fair, Seavey did engage in the lawful transport of local commodities: fruit from Door County, hay and grain from Kewaunee, prostitutes from the Iron Range.

According to Powers: "The *Wanderer* regularly supplied Squeaky Swartz's Frankfort bordello with 'soiled doves.' And after dropping off the fresh faces, Squeaky often loaded up women who'd had the shine worn off working at Squeaky's and transported them to the Soo area, where new clientele eagerly awaited them."

But Seavey would drop anchor in harbors along the way and invite the women to line the deck. In no time rowboats would be making their way to the *Wanderer,* and Seavey was safely offshore to avoid any pesky local authorities.

Seavey's most lucrative business was venison. By several accounts he ran one of the largest poaching operations on the Great Lakes. Allegedly he did battle with Booth Fisheries when the commercial fishing company attempted to horn in on his poaching racket, resulting in a Booth-owned boat going to the bottom with all hands.

There is no disputing that Seavey, a large man for his day, loved a good brawl.

"Seavey heard there was tough fighter in Manistee," recounts a *Milwaukee Journal* article. "The two met in a saloon and agreed to fight. First they drove the bartender and customers out so that they could have more fighting room. All the windows and bar fixtures were smashed when police arrived, just as Seavey knocked out the Manistee bruiser."

"Perhaps his most notorious fight occurred one winter day in 1904 at Frankfort, MI," according to the WUAA. "Mitch Love, rumored to be a professional fighter, battled Dan on the ice of Frankfort Harbor, where a large circle drawn in the snow served as a makeshift ring. The contest, witnessed by some 200 betting fight fans, lasted over two hours until a bruised and battered Love was carted off by his dejected supporters."

It was all fun and games and easy cash—sailing through the night with deer carcasses stuffed in the hold, smashing up waterfront saloons on long winter days, pimping for frontier prostitutes—until his greatest heist, the *Nellie Johnson*, led to the call for Dan Seavey's neck, potentially in a noose.

The imposing US Revenue Service Cutter *Tuscarora*, 178 feet long, gleaming white, the brass of two six-pound cannons shining in the sun, departed Milwaukee in pursuit of Seavey mid-June 1908. Captain Ueberroth set a course to canvass the east shore of Lake Michigan.

"We visited St. Joseph and South Haven, patrolling the river and harbor without finding the vessel. Then we took in Saugatuck, Holland, Grand Haven, Muskegon, Whitehall, Pentwater, and Ludington without a trace."

Ueberroth's biggest concern was having personnel at the life-saving stations tip off Seavey. (It's possible some of those men had enjoyed Seavey's floating bordello when it came to town.)

For more than a week the *Tuscarora* plowed along the lakeshore.

All the while Seavey was hiding in Frankfort, the *Nellie Johnson* moored on a river inland.

Ueberroth finally received notice from the Frankfort station, about the same time Seavey received his.

"We waited all night and had just dropped anchor to communicate again with the life saving station when we sighted the schooner under full sail and with a good stiff breeze sailing directly out into the lake," reported Ueberroth.

Seavey had switched to the *Wanderer* to make his run. For hours the schooner dodged the *Tuscarora*, the steamer pursing at top speed for so long the paint on the smokestack melted.

The Feds closed ranks only when the wind conspired to slow Seavey. Ueberroth ordered a cannon shot across the bow of the *Wanderer*. That ended the chase. Seavey was taken to Chicago in irons.

"The revenue cutter overhauled Seavey in the schooner *Wanderer* seven miles southwest of Frankfort," reported the *Chicago Tribune*, "and sending on board a detachment of marines under arms brought him aboard the cutter and served him with a warrant charging piracy, a crime which is punishable by death."

But instead of piracy, Seavey was charged with "unauthorized removal of a vessel on which he had once been a seaman." Apparently Seavey had sailed on the *Nellie Johnson* years earlier. It saved his neck—that and having a lawyer who knew a good technicality when he saw it. Seavey was released on bond. In no time he was back on the water, wearing a new suit and a big smile.

The charges were later dropped altogether, for reasons unknown. For all we know Seavey won the ship fair and square in a poker game that night in Grand Haven, just as he maintained for the rest of his life.

Commandeering a ship and eluding federal authorities for two weeks only to be set free and made a celebrity could have been Seavey's greatest accomplishment. It wasn't.

"On the theory that it takes a crook to catch a crook, Seavey is appointed a US Marshal and ordered to close down illegal whisky, venison and smuggling on Lake Michigan," according to historian Stonehouse.

He pursued his new job with characteristic gusto. One legend maintains he killed a bootlegger following a brutal fight in a Naubinway tavern by dropping a piano on the man's head.

When the infamous *Wanderer* was destroyed by fire in 1918, Seavey upgraded to a forty-foot motor launch. It's unclear if he continued as a marshal or an outlaw, or both. It should be noted the speedy motor launches were the vehicle of choice for Great Lake rum runners when Prohibition began, just about the time Seavey's schooner burned.

One account states Seavey retired from the water in 1926. Another says he was sailing well into the 1930s.

"Seavey had a soft spot for children and would treat them to fruit from his ship and tales of his many adventures," according to the Wisconsin Maritime Museum. Old-timers in Escanaba relate stories of Seavey buying root beer for the kids when he hit town.

"He wasn't rough talking, he was very mild mannered, quiet. I think he kept his talents as a thief undercover," a ninety-two-year-old Escanaba resident told the *Marquette Monthly* in

2008. "He was an odd guy working on the edge, making a buck wherever he could."

According to the maritime museum, Seavey became religious in his old age and was often seen carrying a Bible around Peshtigo, the town in which he retired.

Seavey died in a Peshtigo nursing home February 14, 1949, an inglorious end to a life fully lived. He was eighty-four. It has been reported he died penniless and lonely. He couldn't have been entirely lonely; his brief obituary in the *Marinette Eagle* notes Seavey had resided in the area for many years with a daughter.

While the truth of Dan Seavey's life and crimes will likely never be revealed, we do know this: At his core Seavey was a master of the lakes, and it's not a stretch to picture the land-bound old sailor gazing from a nursing home window, looking east toward the waters of Green Bay, imagining the roll of the waves and the snap of the sail, the luminescent Milky Way overhead, a dependable schooner underfoot, the humid summer night heavy with scent of kelp, and through the mist, the distant clang of a channel buoy calling him home.

Captain Dan Seavey is buried next to his daughter in Forest Home Cemetery, Marinette.

CHAPTER 8

Valley of the Molls

On Monday evening, April 23, 1934, a reporter for the *Wisconsin State Journal* stood outside the Dane County jail in the shadow of big things. Across the street, the imposing face of St. Raphael's Church towered over him, its steeple paralleled by the state capitol dome one block away, both structures rising high into the cold night sky above Madison, Wisconsin.

About 9:30 p.m. a pair of mud-splattered sedans rolled into the driveway where the reporter was waiting. Five men wielding shotguns bounded from the cars. After coaxing three women from the vehicles, the group moved quickly to the jail entrance.

The front doors were locked. The reporter peppered the group with questions.

"The chiefs are the only ones who do the talking," snapped one of the men, a federal agent. The entourage spun around the building to the residence in back, where Sheriff Fred Finn was caught unaware of his latest guests.

"The girls, all of whom appeared to be still in their teen age," the reporter wrote, "were nattily dressed in puttees and sports attire. They were hungry and haggard after a long day's excitement. Sheriff Finn ordered food prepared for them. They ate heartily."

Finn realized the implications of hosting the three women in his jail. All roads led to Madison now.

The women were placed in the jail's "best" cells while the federal agents deposited a small arsenal of arms and ammunition. Located in the middle of the building, the cells lacked windows for easy escape, unlike the street-side cells, from which prisoners could talk to pedestrians through the windows.

Finn ordered visitors out of the building and positioned two county highway officers with shotguns in the jail office. Two more officers were secreted in the courthouse overlooking the jail entrance. It was everything the sheriff could muster, except to wish out loud that the newspaper wouldn't announce the women's arrival.

"Think there could be a raid?" the reporter asked.

"Well, you can't tell what they will do," Finn responded. "It wouldn't be a pleasant sensation to have five or six of those fellows come here and stick guns in your stomach."

The *Wisconsin State Journal* had its scoop, a big one, and to Finn's dismay, the next morning's headline shouted across all eight columns: "Dillinger Gang Molls Behind Bars Here."

For one year John Dillinger owned the attention of the nation, if not much of the world. From June 1933 to July 1934 Dillinger and his confederates terrorized the Midwest, leaving more than a dozen men dead or wounded in their wake. They stole hundreds of thousands of dollars from at least ten banks, staged spectacular jailbreaks, and knocked over police arsenals at will.

By the spring of 1934, in the dreary reality of the Great Depression, Dillinger's exploits were becoming folklore. At a rustic northern Wisconsin lodge called Little Bohemia, the Dillinger mystique would reach epic proportions.

Dillinger had checked into the lodge with his full accompaniment of well-dressed associates: Homer Van Meter, John "Three Fingered Jack" Hamilton, Tommy Carroll, and the killer's killer himself, Lester Gillis, aka "Baby Face Nelson." Little Bohemia's owner recognized the outlaws. The owner also recognized that each man had bulging armpits, a fashion resulting from carrying .45 caliber handguns in shoulder holsters. Through a daring trip into nearby Mercer and by smuggling messages written in matchbook covers, Little Bohemia's owner secretly notified relatives, who contacted the Chicago bureau of the federal Justice Department.

Dozens of government agents, "G-men," converged on Little Bohemia. Nervous and cold, agents failed to surround the lodge in the pitch-black woods. Chaos erupted as agents opened fire on three Civilian Conservation Corps workers leaving the lodge bar, killing one of the workers and injuring the others. The gang returned fire before escaping through back windows and disappearing into the woods. Later that night, at another resort, Baby Face Nelson shot a federal agent in the head at point-blank range.

Ten hours later, the G-men were still shooting at Little Bohemia, believing they had the gang cornered, when a voice came from the basement.

"We'll come out if you stop firing."

The desperate cries of desperate men it was not. To the horror of the law-abiding world, emerging from Little Bohemia through the early morning haze and tear gas were not the most notorious gangsters of the day, but three young women, two of them dressed in pajamas, and another holding a Boston bull terrier named Rex.

Virtually every corner of the world was talking about the gunfight and Dillinger's escape. At home, President Roosevelt addressed the nation while Congress prepared twelve anti-crime bills.

The botched raid was a problem for the Justice Department. With both Director J. Edgar Hoover and Chicago bureau man Melvin Purvis under pressure to resign, the official Justice Department reports were massaged to say agents shot only the tires of the automobile driven by the conservation workers. To refocus attention on the outlaws, Hoover issued a dramatic "shoot to kill" order with plenty of media attention.

The largest manhunt in history fanned out through five states with five thousand federal, state, and local officers—and countless vigilantes—in tow.

With the *State Journal's* announcement of the three women's arrival began Madison's tenure as the epicenter of Dillinger-induced hysteria. The cocksure outlaws would surely spring their girls from jail, especially since one of the women claimed to be married to a gang member. Dillinger had turned jailbreaks into an art form. Weeks earlier, Dillinger had escaped from an Indiana jail past an army of police and National Guardsmen. Breaking into jail to free the women would be a cinch compared to breaking out. With an arsenal of weapons at the gang's disposal and a man like Baby Face Nelson on hand, a man who delighted in killing cops, Madison's streets would flow red with blood.

The days that followed would be unlike any other.

Getting the women out of Madison would be the best way to avoid bloodshed, but the city was home to the federal court where the women would be arraigned. Sheriff Finn did the next best thing. If he could not rid the city of the women, at least he could rid the jail of them. The gang would be greeted by a shower of bullets if they tried to fight their way in, while the women would be held somewhere else in the city.

But where?

Finn smuggled his three prisoners into the last place John Dillinger would ever be caught dead or alive: St. Raphael's Catholic Church, just across the street from the jail.

Next, Finn placed floodlights in the jail's driveway and around the county garage to keep the area lit through the night.

J. Edgar Hoover, his grip firmly on the Madison situation, had no intention of enduring another Little Bohemia fiasco. Federal agents began descending on Madison from St. Paul, Milwaukee, and Chicago.

"A picked squad of the best sharpshooters in the department of justice was speeding to Wisconsin as the government net was drawing closer on the fleeing gang chieftain and his aides," reported the *Capital Times*.

"Authorities here were guarding against any possibility of raid tonight by Dillinger or his associates. Guards armed with machine guns, riot guns and shotguns paced the corridors surrounding the cells where the trio of teen-aged 'molls' rested after an all-night journey from the Vilas County jail."

Eventually, the women were returned to jail as federal agents reinforced the facility.

The identity of the mysterious "molls," as the newspapers enjoyed calling the women, was limited to brief, yet alluring, physical descriptions:

"Marian Marr, a comely brunet in lounging pajamas, is about 5 feet 6 inches tall. She is said to be the wife of one of the gangsters.

"Ann Southern, a blond of the Mae West type, appeared to be about 5 feet 4 inches tall, weighing about 130 pounds.

"Following these two was Rose Ancker, a petite auburn-haired girl, 5 feet 3 inches tall, about 110 pounds. She appeared to be the best looking of the trio."

On Tuesday afternoon, April 24, the day after the women arrived, a bulletin confirmed Madison's worst fear. Johnny was on his way.

"Men believed to be John Dillinger and three henchmen were reported heading in the direction of Madison at 8 o'clock this morning. In Milwaukee, four men armed with machine guns were sighted in a big car speeding out of the city along Highway 18."

Federal agents hit the streets in "heavily armed" vehicles. Madison police stopped dark sedans at random.

At noon, a salesman reported seeing three "roughly dressed" men stopped at a crossroads northwest of the city. One of the men was sitting in a large black sedan while the other two were intently studying a highway map at the side of the road. The salesman picked the photograph of John Hamilton as the man sitting in the car.

Agents and county deputies moved into position, girding their loins for a do or die battle with the most notorious gang in the land.

A six-hour search produced no "roughly dressed" men.

The Madison common council moved quickly, albeit quietly, to transfer funds to the police department. The council had previously balked at the police department's request for a machine gun. Now the council hoped to make the appropriation in secret—until the *Capital Times* reported on its front page that $2,000 would be invested in a machine gun, bullets, a bullet-proof vest, and an armored car.

The three women were to be arraigned at noon Wednesday before the federal court commissioner. Fearing an ambush on the way to the court office, officials scheduled the arraignment inside the jail. Moments before, the court commissioner assured reporters that the hearing, like any other in Madison, would be open to the public. Reporters approached the jail entrance.

"The federal government is running this hearing, and I've been given orders to not admit nobody," announced Sheriff Finn, who had been unceremoniously dispatched to enforce the new rules according to J. Edgar Hoover. Finn held the crowd at bay, telling reporters that even he had "not seen the girls since they were brought here."

Reporters saw the women being led to the jail office and rushed a window. The shades were drawn promptly.

Inside, nearly a dozen armed guards crowded into the small jail office for the arraignment. A score of others patrolled surrounding corridors.

Bail was set at fifty thousand dollars each. A grand jury would convene May 7.

That night, "Dillinger-conscious" agents roamed Madison streets in search of a "big sedan" carrying four men, reported to have circled the county jail four times between 11 p.m. and 2 a.m.

In the center of the fear and the frenzy and the shotguns remained the women. The trio had been offering misinformation from the moment they walked out of Little Bohemia. Authorities struggled with the basics of their identity, including their real names. One maintained she was Ann Southern, a popular actress of the day.

Federal agents knew how to break the toughest of men. They went to work on the women.

"Valuable information regarding John Dillinger and his gang slipped from the lips of their three deserted feminine consorts today," *United Press* reported.

"The bravado in which they displayed when they were forced out of Little Bohemia lodge by a barrage of machine gun bullets and tear gas was gone. The stubborn resistance with which they first met questioning has broken down. Bit by bit the gangsters' girls offered information, bargaining for sleep and rest. Each further revelation only brought more inquiry."

Marian Marr told agents that she had been married only two weeks to one of the gangsters—she wouldn't say which one—and had been spending her honeymoon at Little Bohemia. "Gangster's Bride Spends Honeymoon Alone in Cell," blared the *Wisconsin State Journal*. "County Jail Is Honeymoon Hotel to Gangster Girl," countered the *Capital Times*.

According to one account, "For a dozen adventure-packed days, three girls traveled and consorted with a quintet of the 'baddest men' on the American continent, five men led by John Dillinger on a trail of murder that has cost this country more than a million dollars.

"You would, perhaps, think the three girls who, apparently voluntarily, followed these desperados would be 'bad' in more ways than one. But two of them don't even drink or smoke!

WISCONSIN HISTORICAL SOCIETY

Little Bohemia, circa 1930 (Whi-53880).

"Federal agents who have spent three days and four nights questioning the trio have found that two of the girls—blond, shapely Ann Southern and the petite red-head, Rose Ancker— neither drink nor smoke. The other member of the trio of 'molls' is Marian Marr, who claimed to be married to one of their gangster companions."

Marr, apparently, did drink and smoke.

The *Wisconsin State Journal* featured "Ann Southern," whose sister arrived in Madison with an attorney:

She says, to the outside world, 'My name's Ann Southern, the movie actress,' but her real name's Delaney, she's 21, her home is in St. Paul and she's sorry to have brought 'all this trouble' to her family.

The blonde Ann and her attractive brunette sister, clad in a neat blue suit with white trimmings, embraced, wept a bit and talked about family affairs when the two met for the first time since the three girls were deserted by the fleeing gangsters.

Ann, it was reported, seemed quite concerned over her mother and the effect upon the latter's health caused by her daughter's plight.

Ann Southern, or Ann Delaney, would later be identified as Jean Compton. Her sister was married to Dillinger pal Pat Reilly. Delaney's attorney declared that her association with the gang was innocent.

A "comfortable" sum of money was left "to provide comforts during her incarceration."

Agents discovered that Marian Marr was Helen Gillis, wife of Lester Gillis, "Baby Face Nelson." Far from being a new bride, she had been married to the killer for six years and was a mother of two children whose whereabouts were unknown.

The extent of the women's complicity with the gang's activities remained a mystery. The prisoners admitted only one thing. They missed Rex, the dog.

The panic eased somewhat as Dillinger was thought to be in Minneapolis, Chicago, or England. Sheriff Finn's wife regularly entertained the women in their jail cells, although his children were still escorted to school by deputies.

On April 30, another wave of hysteria swept the city. Baby Face Nelson, who had been on the lam by himself in northern Wisconsin (he housed himself for two days with an unimpressed Chippewa Indian named Ole Catfish) was spotted in two places at once. In side-by-side columns, the *Capital Times* reported that Baby Face was one of four gunmen involved in a skirmish with Chicago police, while another bulletin placed him outside Madison in a stolen car: "Posse Hunts Nelson Near City."

"Police at Watertown today received a report that 'Baby Face' Nelson had been seen early this morning by a farmer on a side road."

A district attorney in a neighboring county joined the fray by claiming that he had tailed Nelson the night before, his suspicions aroused by a dark-colored sedan with weeds obscuring the license plate. Two men also reported a car "somewhat" matching Nelson's driving on a downtown Madison street.

On May 19, a grand jury indicted each woman on charges of harboring a fugitive. Technically, the women were guilty as charged, but authorities believed the trio had been led astray. A week later, after more than a month behind bars, the women were given a suspended sentence and placed on probation.

"I don't think you are a bad girl," the judge told Marie Conforti, aka Rose Ancker. "I know you're not. You just got into some bad company."

He turned to the crowded courtroom. "I am satisfied this mere girl had no knowledge these men were gangsters," the judge said. "I am convinced she would not have jeopardized her own life by associating with dangerous criminals."

Each woman was required to return to Chicago and report to a probation officer weekly for eighteen months.

After the proceedings, the *Wisconsin State Journal* asked the women how they enjoyed their stay in Madison.

Conforti: "I'm saying nothing."

Compton: "What I've seen of Madison, I don't like."

Gillis: "I hope I never see this state again."

The *Capital Times* won the final newspaper battle by assigning its society reporter, Selma Sable Parker, to cover the women's departure from the city. Before catching a train to Chicago, the four women went shopping around the Capital Square and enjoyed beer and potato salad at a drug store. Enigmatic as ever, the women sounded a decidedly different tone, praising Madison as a beautiful lake city full of "nice shops."

"Turn a woman loose, and she's bound to go shopping!" Parker wrote. The items bought by women "proved their excellent taste."

"Don't call us 'molls' when you write your story," pleaded Conforti. "We hate that name. We're not 'molls' or 'gang girls.' After we've reported to the probation judge in Chicago, we're going right out to look for jobs and start all over."

Still, questions lingered after the three women waved goodbye from the Chicago & Northwestern train depot: Gangster "molls," or good women keeping bad company?

In less than two weeks, Jean Compton, aka Ann Southern, reunited with Tommy Carroll. She was with him when he was gunned down in Waterloo, Iowa, on June 7. Compton was arrested and sentenced to a year in prison for violating parole.

By the end of June, Marie Conforti, aka Rose Ancker, and Homer Van Meter were renting a room in Calumet City, Illinois. On August 23, Van Meter was killed in a gunfight with St. Paul police. The "dark, exotic little" Marie Conforti was arrested in Minneapolis the next day. Conforti served a year in prison for violating parole.

On November 27, 1934, Helen Gillis and Baby Face Nelson were spotted by police driving a stolen car near Barrington, Illinois. In the ensuing gunfight, Baby Face killed two federal agents and was fatally wounded. Helen Gillis left her husband's body at a local cemetery. She was arrested two days later and sentenced to a year in prison for violating parole. Helen Gillis died in 1987.

CHAPTER 9

Doomed: The Winter Dance Party of 1959

As he sped out of Hurley on southbound US 51, the Iron County sheriff must have wondered if he would find any survivors. A trucker had notified the sheriff's department that a group of men—without hats, gloves, or winter coats—was seen standing outside a stranded bus ten or fifteen miles south of town. Any person exposed to Arctic cold without proper clothes or shelter would be in serious, life-threatening trouble. Every minute that passed made it more likely the people stuck out on Highway 51 were succumbing to exposure.

It was the early hours of February 1, 1959.

One mile north of Pine Lake, the sheriff found the darkened bus on the roadside. Stepping inside with his flashlight, the sheriff was greeted by a group of pale and sick young men, some huddled together under blankets. One person couldn't stand up.

Maybe the only thing that kept the group alive was the fact that they had no idea how close they were to dying. They were musicians—rock-and-rollers—on their way to Appleton, Wisconsin, after a show in Duluth, Minnesota. A number of the young men hailed from Texas, another was from southern California. None had ever experienced weather like this. The sheriff had heard of one of the singers. His name was Buddy Holly.

Buddy Holly rocketed up the music charts in 1957 with songs that instantly became a part of the American songbook, including "That'll Be the Day," "Peggy Sue," and "Oh Boy." Second only to Elvis as the voice of the new rock-and-roll phenomenon, Holly was huge overseas, too, directly influencing a generation of young English rockers from whom a dynamic foursome would emerge a few years later.

Holly spent 1958 touring nonstop at home and abroad, yet by the end of the year he was virtually penniless thanks to his manager. He was also expecting a baby with his wife, Maria, and had begun plans to create his own record company and recording studio.

Holly reluctantly agreed to headline the Winter Dance Party of 1959. The tour was comprised of up-and-coming talent beneath Holly's stature as an established artist, but it offered one thing he desperately needed as the new year dawned: cash.

"The only reason Buddy went on that tour was because he was broke—flat broke," Waylon Jennings, Holly's bass player on the ill-fated tour, would say years later. "He didn't want to go but he had to make some money."

The tour of the upper Midwest was organized by General Artists Corporation (GAC), a shoestring outfit headed by a druggist who sold records from his pharmacies and cared little for rock-and-roll. The tour schedule established by GAC was absurd. The group had to endure daily bus travels spanning Iowa, Minnesota, and Wisconsin. GAC accepted any offer that came along and filled the dates regardless of the distance involved. Holly was appalled when he received the schedule. He told GAC he wanted out, but it was too late, the deal was done.

Expectant dad Holly reluctantly said goodbye to Maria—both had experienced premonitions in the days leading up to the tour—and headed to Milwaukee where the Winter Dance Party was set to debut January 23, 1959.

The musicians unloaded their equipment at Milwaukee's George Devine's ballroom on Wisconsin Avenue, wary of the headlines appearing at every newsstand across the city: "Snowstorms grip Midwest with Arctic cold to follow."

The Upper Midwest was experiencing the deadliest winter in decades. Temperatures had plunged at the start of the year and remained below zero for more than three weeks straight; then a blizzard dumped thirteen inches of snow on the region in late January, claiming the lives of thirty-three people. A weather emergency was declared. Milwaukee residents were still digging out from one winter storm as the Winter Dance Party of 1959 made its debut. Holly opened his set with a new song written by folk singer Paul Clayton titled "Gotta Travel On." The *Milwaukee Sentinel* reported:

Where Entertainment Reigns Supreme

The RIVERSIDE BALLROOM

JOSEPH W. BECKER
1700 MAIN STREET
Phone 577
GREEN BAY, WIS.

MICHAEL BIE COLLECTION

Postcard for the Riverside Ballroom in Green Bay, Wis. (undated).

It was crazy, daddy—the goings-on Friday at George Devine's Million Dollar Ballroom. Nearly 6,000 young people turned out to hear such rock 'n' roll stars as Buddy Holly and the Crickets, Big Bopper, Dion and the Belmonts and Ritchie Valens. If you haven't heard them, you haven't lived, man.

It's obvious the Big Beat still has a hold on the kids and it takes steady nerves to withstand the sound. Backed by the Crickets—two young guitarists and a drummer—Buddy Holly rocked his beanpole figure on stage, clutched his little guitar against his loud red coat and jerked his way through "Peggy Sue." His voice was scarcely audible over the raucous guitars, but he itchy-twitched in grand style, and that's what the kids wanted.

Electric guitars boomed through two loudspeakers with the force of two symphony orchestras in full sway, and the twitching rock 'n' rollers invoked screams that surely melted the snow on the roof of the ballroom.

Far from it. Holly grabbed the wad of cash—he was paid about five hundred dollars after every show—stuffed it into the sweaty shirt pocket under his suit jacket and walked outside where the winds off Lake Michigan felt like shards of glass on his exposed skin. Temperatures were below zero.

Making matters worse, GAC had accepted the lowest bid for the bus service. Not surprisingly, there were problems with the substandard vehicle. The musicians crammed into the bus and some took to the luggage racks to sleep, soon realizing that the heating system was woefully inadequate—if it was working at all.

"Such lousy old buses," Holly's guitarist Tommy Allsup would recall bitterly decades later. "They weren't really buses. They were jokes."

Bronx native Dion DiMucci, in an interview for the 2004 book *The Day the Music Died*, was more direct: "It wasn't a bus, it was a piece of shit."

Drummer Carl Bunch's toes began to tingle from the cold.

Traveling on two-lane roads covered with ice and drifting snow, the tour plunged into the initial leg of its schedule: Kenosha's Eagles Ballroom to Mankato, Minnesota, 350 miles;

Mankato to Eau Claire's Fournier's Ballroom, 170 miles; Eau Claire to Montevideo in western Minnesota, 230 miles.

In Eau Claire temperatures dropped to twenty-five degrees below zero.

"Buddy roared through seven songs" at Fournier's Ballroom January 26, according to biographer Ellis Amburn: "Gotta Travel On," "Peggy Sue," "That'll Be the Day," "Heartbeat," "Be Bop a Lula," "Whole Lotta Shakin' Goin' On," and "It Doesn't Matter Anymore."

"After the show, Buddy, Ritchie, and the Bopper ate dinner at Sammy's Pizza," according to Amburn. "Carl Bunch discovered that he'd lost his gray and black stage clothes, which meant the musicians would now have to wear their one remaining costume, the brown tweed, until their clothes were filthy."

The tour provided hotel lodging when the schedule allowed. Other nights the group, still wet with perspiration following their performances (and loading their equipment), had to endure a grueling ride on a freezing bus stinking of diesel fumes, body odor, sardines, and booze. It was impossible to sleep. At first, the musicians endured the conditions by singing and placing bets on guitar contests between Holly and Dion. Within days, however, the group's discomfort began to deteriorate to treacherous levels as colds and flu began to waylay the musicians. Holly almost collapsed backstage at the Montevideo show. Carl Bunch began losing the feeling in his feet.

The tour trudged on to St. Paul, Minnesota, Davenport and Fort Dodge, Iowa.

Another bus was brought in following the St. Paul show. Like the first, the heater was on the blink. Bunch began having trouble coordinating his feet. The musicians resorted to wearing light clothing after the shows and huddling under blankets in small groups, usually with a bottle to help tolerate the cold.

"Holly and I used to climb under a blanket together to keep warm," Dion wrote in his autobiography. The two would sing "Teenager in Love." Jennings and J. P. Richardson, the Big Bopper, drank vodka under another blanket and composed country songs.

From Fort Dodge it was 370 miles north to Duluth, Minnesota. Valens phoned his manager at a stop along the way. After describing the conditions, the young Chicano singer was told to leave the tour immediately and return to Los Angeles. He opted to stay, the thrill of the shows outweighing the misery of the bus.

That night at the Duluth armory a young Robert Zimmerman, later known as Bob Dylan, angled close to the stage and was mesmerized by Holly. Dylan recounted that night when he accepted a Grammy Award in 1998.

The group started the 340-mile trip from Duluth to Appleton on US Highway 2, a concrete thread winding through the heart of the remote Chequamegon National Forest, an area on the razor's edge of the Arctic front slashing down across Lake Superior. Wind chills were estimated at forty degrees below zero.

Winter Dance Party advertisement,
Eau Claire, Wis.

Turning south on US 51 shortly after midnight, February 1, the bus approached a hill fifteen miles south of Hurley when disaster struck. The bus died.

"We didn't know enough to be afraid, or what a midwinter night by the side of the road meant," Dion said in his autobiography.

Unprepared and sickly, members of the tour party were trapped in the worst possible predicament. The temperature inside the bus was roughly the same as outdoors, with pounding winds sending drafts through the windows. Frozen tree limbs were snapping like twigs in the wind, crashing to the ground in the forest surrounding the group.

The group began burning newspapers in the aisle for heat, which provided only a few fleeting moments of relief. Carl Bunch was unable to move his legs at all. One backup musician began to panic. "We can't stay in this bus," he begged the others. "They'll read about us in the paper tomorrow."

They stayed put, fortunately. Whatever shelter the bus provided was better than attempting to walk for help, quite likely a lethal mistake had it been attempted. Some of the musicians stepped outside hoping to flag down a vehicle. At that time of night in remote Iron County with conditions being what they were, not a soul was traveling.

"I'm looking for traffic," the road manager recounted in an interview. "Nothing. I'm worried about it. The kids in the back were freezing."

The group was in serious danger. With no other option, the men grabbed their instruments and began a jam session in the bus to stay active.

Carl Bunch prayed for deliverance.

After an hour, the group saw the headlights of a semi-truck approaching through the darkness. They hurried off the bus and into the middle of the road. The trucker slowed enough to maneuver around the men but never stopped. Dejected, the musicians filed back on the bus.

"We just sat there and froze," Tommy Allsup said. Holly and Dion told their life stories to one another under a blanket, passing time "through the dark hours while we waited for something to happen," according to Dion.

After two hours on the roadside, the Iron County sheriff arrived. The trucker had notified the police when he reached town. The group was shuttled, a few people at a time, back to Hurley's Club Carnival Cafe, a strip joint on notorious Silver Street, where they were fed breakfast—except for the group's black bus driver, who had to eat in the county garage.

Carl Bunch was rushed to Grand View Hospital in Ironwood, Michigan.

Despite the ordeal and the fact that the bus was shot, GAC instructed the group to fulfill the Green Bay performance that night. The 1:30 p.m. matinee at Appleton's Cinderella Ballroom was cancelled. Members of the entourage boarded the 11:30 a.m. Chicago Northwestern train out of Hurley and made it to Green

Bay with time to spare before the 8 p.m. show at the Riverside Ballroom. They reportedly checked into a downtown hotel, most likely the Northland.

It was the tenth performance for the Winter Dance Party, Holly's second-to-last performance. Tickets were 90 cents in advance, $1.25 day of show. "No jeans or slacks permitted, and no intoxicating beverages will be served."

Roughly twenty-two hundred young people crowded under the arched ceilings of the Riverside, "where entertainment reigns supreme," according to the postcards sold at the ticket window. WDUZ radio jock Bill Walters emceed. Frankie Sardo opened the show followed by Dion, the Big Bopper, and headliner Holly, who again opened his set with the country song "Gotta Travel On," which would become one of the biggest hits of 1959 as recorded by Billy Grammer. On that sub-zero January evening, certainly the irony was not lost on a homesick Holly as he sang, "That chilly wind will soon begin and I'll be on way/Going home to stay."

The group was desperately looking forward to a scheduled day off after the Green Bay show to recuperate from their harrowing experience. Much to their dismay, GAC had added a show in Clear Lake, Iowa, 357 miles away. It was twenty degrees below zero when they boarded the latest tour bus. The group departed Green Bay on US 41, rolling past the exit for Austin Straubel Airport, where a North Central Airlines flight would arrive at 2:20 p.m. with the new and largely unknown head coach of the Green Bay Packers, Vince Lombardi. A news conference to introduce the coach was scheduled at the Hotel Northland.

Three hundred miles to Clear Lake, Iowa, and to the group's disgust, the bus heater was not functioning as it sputtered across Wisconsin. At a pit stop in Prairie du Chien, Richardson returned to the bus with a sleeping bag purchased at a sporting goods store. "Man, I'm gonna be warm tonight," the Big Bopper bragged to the others.

After the evening performance at the Surf Ballroom in Clear Lake, the tour was scheduled for a ten-hour, 440-mile ride to Moorhead, Minnesota. GAC had arranged for a school bus to get them there.

Buddy Holly had enough. He chartered a small plane to reach Moorhead. A warm hotel room, clean sheets, and hot food would await him there, and he could take the group's dirty laundry for proper cleaning. Valens and Richardson, who was feeling ill, asked to fly along.

Moments after takeoff, the plane crashed into an Iowa cornfield, killing the three musicians and the pilot.

CHAPTER 10

Pancakes from Space

Joe Simonton lived on a farm four miles west of Eagle River in the remote North Woods region of Wisconsin best known, if known at all outside Vilas County, for tall pines and placid lakes. For thirty years Simonton enjoyed the simple life of raising chickens and providing plumbing and auctioneering services to folks in the area. Most knew Joe as the guy who played Santa Claus for the annual Eagle River Chamber of Commerce holiday pageant.

That changed April 18, 1961.

It was a Tuesday, about 11 a.m., and the sixty-year-old Simonton was inside his farmhouse having a bite to eat when he heard a noise resembling knobby tires on concrete. Stepping outside, Simonton was greeted by the glare of a flying saucer, twelve feet high by thirty feet wide, hovering five feet from the ground. A hatch opened on the side of the vehicle revealing three men. One of the men, dressed in a black two-piece suit, held a jug made of the same bright metallic material as the vehicle. The man waved the jug at Simonton to indicate it was empty.

Simonton took the jug inside, filled it with water, and returned to the spaceship. The visitors were about five feet tall, Simonton reckoned, and weighed 125 pounds or so. They were clean shaven with swarthy complexions. Kind of like Italians, he thought.

The three visitors did not speak. Simonton noticed the interior of the spaceship was wrought-iron black with a number of instrument panels, and he could hear a low humming sound.

One of the men was cooking on a grill, and when Simonton pointed toward the food, the cook, dressed in black with a narrow red stripe along the pants, gave him three small pancakes.

Following the goodwill exchange, water for pancakes, the hatch closed, the saucer zoomed away, and that was that. The encounter lasted less than five minutes.

Simonton kept the visit to himself. Who would believe such a thing? He had his Santa job to uphold, for goodness sake. When the holidays rolled around what parents would allow their kids to visit a known crackpot?

On the other hand, Joe knew what he saw, and he had no ulterior motives, no plans to sell space pancakes or charge admission to the barnyard or anything of the sort.

Unable to continue to bear silent witness after a day or two, Simonton did the most reasonable thing he could think of and contacted the Vilas County sheriff's department, which dispatched Sergeant Adolph Mussatti and Deputy Marv Elliot to the scene. Clear-eyed, serious, certain of the details, Joe gave his statement to the men, pointing to a circular depression in the yard where the craft had hovered. Elliot and Mussatti noticed a goat tied to a post in the same spot. "And look at this," Simonton added, carefully opening a kerchief. It was a small pancake, black with tiny holes as if it had been left on the griddle too long. Joe said he had eaten one and it tasted like cardboard.

After exchanging silent glances with one another, the officers thanked Simonton for calling and departed.

In Eagle River the following Saturday morning, a fine spring day in the northland, the kind of day that clears any remnants of cabin fever, word started to get around Mickleberry's Restaurant. Seated in one of the booths were Dan Satran, editor of the *Vilas County News Review*, District Attorney Calvin Burton, who had heard the story in the courthouse, and two men from the advertising department of the *Chicago Sun Times*. Intrigued by the rumor—and heck, it was such a nice, warm, sunny day anyway—the group piled into a car and headed to Joe's farm, Satran dutifully carrying a reporter's notebook.

The saucer was "brighter than chrome," Simonton described in virtually the same detail as he done with the sheriff's deputies. He had filled the jug with water and brought it back to the open hatch of the spaceship. "It appeared one of the men in the ship was frying food on a flameless grill of some sort."

Simonton was offended when smirks appeared on the men's faces. He wouldn't continue if they weren't going to take him seriously. Reassured by the group, he resumed.

The hatch had snapped shut after the space travelers gave him the pancakes. The craft was machined so smoothly he could barely tell where the door had been after it closed. The ship took off rapidly in a blast of air that bowed the pine trees.

"When it took off, it really went. It went up, slow and even, about fifteen feet, and then in two seconds it was so far away I couldn't see it."

Back at the *News Review* office, Satran transcribed his notes, pipe firmly in jaw, while the group debated whether any of the downstate newspapers or the wire services would care to use the story at all. On a flyer Satran sent the story to his contacts in Milwaukee. The *Sun Times* guys said it might get picked up by their paper, too.

"Flying Saucer's Crew Landed to Fill Jug, State Man Reports" appeared the next day, Sunday, on the front page of the *Milwaukee Journal*. By Monday morning the story had taken on a life of its own through the news services of the Associated Press, United Press International, and *Stars and Stripes,* ensuring that the story of aliens landing in Eagle River, Wisconsin, was appearing in media reports around the world. Follow-up reporting quoted the Vilas County sheriff: "Joe really believes everything he says and he isn't a drinking man. He talks sensibly." And local editor Satran further vouched for Simonton's standing in the community, "If you took a vote around here, most people would say Simonton's story is authentic."

Satran devoted his next column in the *Vilas County News Review* to the hubbub:

But if it had not been a nice day for a drive—and if we had not teamed up with men interested in the novelty of the report, chances are the hundreds of thousands of people who heard about it over the weekend—never would have known the name of Joe Simonton.

The story was not a hoax perpetrated in the name of publicity—although in the light of hindsight, it is obvious some good publicity value was achieved by Eagle River.

On page three of the *Chicago Sun Times*, the story of the flying saucer visit included references to Eagle River as, "this famous resort town," and "the report by Joe Simonton replaced talk of the upcoming onrush of summer vacationers."

Identifying Eagle River with the readers as a famous resort town certainly is helpful.

Eagle River had its moment of publicity glory—and we are certain long years from now, there will be times when it will be mentioned again—when we'll reminisce about the "big story" about the pancakes from outer space.

Response to the story was predictable. Reports of UFO sightings spiked, letters poured into the Eagle River Post Office, and flying saucer gimmicks sprang up all over town.

On a farm near the barely there community of Sugar Camp, members of the Lorbetske family watched a saucer-shaped object moving above the forest. It did not look like a helicopter or airplane, they told the sheriff. "I wouldn't have called you," Brent Lorbetske told the sheriff's department, "but others saw it too." The family matriarch, who was also the Sugar Camp town chairman, was in the barn milking a cow and missed the excitement.

Jack Long of Boulder Junction wryly proclaimed himself a member of the Vilas County Saucer Observation Corps and mounted a Civil War–era cannon on the roof of his grocery store. (He successfully landed a photo in the *News Review*.) The Eagle River bakery sold flying saucer cupcakes, and the gas station invited aliens to "fill 'er up."

Simonton said most of the thousand or so letters he received seemed sincere. "I've got so many letters, I'll be kept busy just answering them. I even got one today from Australia. And I don't know when I'll get around to answering them. I haven't been able to work for three weeks now and I'm going to have to start making some money." He added that he was "irked by some reporters making fun of the situation and laughing. I'm happy to give information to them if they are sincerely interested."

One writer wondered if the "cosmic cookies" might have had some value, galactically speaking: "Had the thought occurred to anyone that the three disks were not cookies, but money? It's been said often enough that thirst will drive a person to trade everything he has for a jug of water. Maybe the 'cookie' [Simonton] ate could have bought some small planet or perhaps even Mars."

Most telling was Joe's comment to the *News Review*: "If it happened again, I don't think I'd tell anybody about it." Nevertheless, he was quick to add, "I don't care what anybody else believes. I just know what I saw."

He believed, apparently—so much that he gave one of the spare pancakes to local circuit judge Frank Carter, who sent the artifact to retired Major Donald Keyhoe, director of the National Investigating Committee on Aerial Phenomena in Washington, D.C. But the group, which had accused the Air Force of concealing information on UFOs, returned the pancake without analysis. A researcher from Northwestern University took it from there and forwarded the pancake to the physics lab at Wright Patterson Air Force Base. The results came back at the end of June.

The test showed the object was made of flour, sugar, salt, and cooking oil.

"Simonton says his space story was confirmed by the length of time it took to process the cake," reported the *Three Lakes News*, telling the newspaper, "The analysis took two months instead of a week or 10 days which they told me it would take when they took the cake from me."

A more detailed report supposedly was coming at a later date, which Simonton said further supported his story because the lab "failed to give me the full report." There is no indication, at least not publicly, of a more detailed report ever being delivered; if it was, Simonton never mentioned it.

Simonton's pancakes from space story remains Wisconsin's most famous claim of alien encounters (if not merely an encounter with Italians in a flying saucer). In today's world a cottage industry related to UFOs and/or alien contact exists, with Internet sites, radio and television programs, books, conventions, and much more devoted to the topic. In Wisconsin an annual event called UFO Daze is held on the shores of Long Lake near the edge of the Kettle Moraine State Forest. The gathering is the swap meet for true believers. Instead of swapping car parts or antique coins, the attendees happily share personal accounts of life with aliens. Like a man named Don, a frequent flyer who began traveling aboard alien spacecrafts at age two, "give or take six months," according to his recollections. The aliens gave Don "implants" to monitor his whereabouts. The implants expired a week before Christmas 1998.

"The speed of their craft is 48 to 52 light years an hour," Don explained to a writer. "They come over me and they put down a blue beam of light so extremely bright that you would go blind instantly if you look at it, but it will not illuminate anything, and I'm taken aboard their ship.

"I've had 68 scheduled flights and 12 non-scheduled flights."

Standing among the hundred or so people milling around Benson's Hideaway tavern on Long Lake you'll grow accustomed to hearing conversations about "shadow people," "reptilians" (bad aliens), and "grays" (good aliens, except for a few bad apples). This scenic area in Fond du Lac County has had its share of UFO sightings through the years. Hideaway owner Bill Benson has a binder to prove it, filled with pages of photos showing strange lights above the forest, as well as a crop circle in a nearby field. He is not a true believer, but truly believes that UFO Daze is good for business, so for more than two decades he has hosted the gathering and served a ton of the Hideaway's homemade pizzas.

In addition to the twenty-five or so true believers who attend, dozens more are curious, and even more are weekend campers looking for a good party.

"When I had my implants they could locate me an hour before they hit the sun's gravitational pull," Don said. "Most people think it's a nighttime situation. It is not. It's day or night, whenever they need you.

"I have been taken straight through a stone wall that was four feet thick. They have taken me through three floors of a building. They have taken me out of a whole group of military people while I was in service and everybody said, 'We were talking to you and all of a sudden all that was there was your clothing.'"

"On my last trip aboard the craft before my implants expired," Don said, "I asked to see the *Titanic*. They took me under the ocean and we talked to the creatures of the deep . . . and I got to see the *Titanic*."

An organization called Lightside, which meets monthly in an Oshkosh Goodwill store, also speaks openly of life with aliens. Lightside member Bonnie Meyer has written about her experiences in *Alien Contact: The Messages They Bring.*

"We all have had benevolent sightings and contacts with highly advanced spiritual aliens," said one Lightside member. Meyer is an exceptional "channeler," according to her peers. "Through channeling we became reacquainted with our ET contacts, as we come here without full memory. The ET team that we work with lives on a ship that we have nicknamed the Peace Ship. The Peace Ship is roughly the size of Chicago and circles the Earth just outside our atmosphere."

It is said Joe Simonton never once joked about his story. Not a wink. If it was a prank, he never let on. Like the folks who gather today to talk openly about their lives with extraterrestrials, Simonton seemingly believed what he said. The one inconsistency, it must be pointed out, is Simonton's assertion that he wished he had never told anyone. He did accept invitations to tell his story in the years following, once renting a tuxedo to speak before a UFO convention.

Joe Simonton died in 1972 at the age of seventy-one.

"A man who brought a lot of happiness to Eagle River area youngsters—and a story which circled the globe about a pancake from outer space died here Monday," began the front page article in the *Vilas County News Review*. "His image as a jovial Santa Claus, and his story about the pancake, should keep him remembered for many years to come."

The article detailed once again Simonton's claim of pancake-wielding visitors from space, noting that he never once cracked a smile when he told the story to the curious.

"He was more enthusiastic about his role as the community Santa Claus. He appeared in many Chamber of Commerce parades riding on the fire truck through the main street. He was also towed in sleds behind snowmobiles as Santa took advantage of this new fangled invention.

"Over a 15 year span he listened to hundreds of youngsters, many bashful, some in tears, as they told him what they wanted for Christmas. In recent years he walked with a heavy limp and a cane as health problems beset him. Some thought he used too much rouge and didn't appear quite as authentic as he once did. But he lived long enough so he never had to face the prospect of a Christmas in which he did not play the role of the most important man of the Yule season."

CHAPTER 11

Vanished: The Enduring Mystery of Leo Burt

T he revolution, it seemed, was at hand. At the state university in Kent, Ohio, national guardsmen opened fire on students protesting the Vietnam War, killing four and wounding nine others. On the University of Wisconsin campus in Madison, where the first organized opposition to the war had its genesis in the 1960s, the backlash following Kent State was virtually combustible. It was May 1970, nearly a decade since those early teach-ins were held at the UW and what had come of it? The Vietnam War was expanding into Cambodia and American soldiers were shooting citizens at home.

Madison had witnessed its share of violence through the 1960s, and from both sides of the barricades. Police harbored no hesitation in using batons on protestors, thus converting otherwise peaceful activists into raging radicals, while anti-war mobs routinely smashed storefronts and hurled bricks to the extent it

seemed to be raining debris, earning the UW campus the dubi-
ous nickname Plywood U.

Word of the Kent State shootings escalated the tension in
Madison to a tipping point. As one observer put it, it was like
throwing gasoline on an open fire.

"The stakes are very high now," proclaimed the *Daily Cardinal,* the UW student newspaper. "We are no longer protesting
a single war but an attack on both Southeast Asian people and
the people of the United States. The issues have been reduced to
one: survival." The paper called for revolution, a word overused
in the day, but this time it seemed to resonate: "We must strike
and strike hard—into the community and on our campus to
turn the tide raging so viciously against us."

In the night following Kent State, on the steps of the UW
Memorial Union, thousands of students were worked into a frenzy
by local and national protest leaders. At the direction of the speak-
ers, the crowd began making its way to campus buildings deemed
undesirable—Sterling Hall, which was home to the Army Math
Research Center, and the ROTC office, among others—breaking
windows and setting fires along the way. At a campus supermar-
ket loathed by students for inflated prices, a fire was started in
the Twinkies section and began raging out of control. Celebrants
danced around the burning building as a garage band played
next door. Battle lines formed at the foot of Bascom Hill. Police,
equipped with monstrous-looking bug-eyed gas masks, began
launching tear gas canisters into the crowd, followed by a rifle

volley of rubber bullets. Protesters dropped in agony. In the chaos it was impossible to know if the rounds were rubber or not. It was not implausible that protestors were being shot dead considering what had transpired at Kent State. The crowd began fleeing across the library mall back to the student union, trampling those already on the ground and causing more to fall like dominoes in the stampede. The sheriff's department had arrived in force, delivered by a caravan of trucks parked along Langdon Street in front of the student union. The protestors were flanked by Madison police on one side and Dane County deputies on the other. Those not speedy or lucky enough to slip through the gauntlet were clubbed.

Dodging police batons in the melee was a twenty-two-year-old reporter for the *Daily Cardinal*. Equipped with his own gas mask, which endeared him not one bit to the authorities, he made his way to the Union where he tried to present a media badge to deputies. That was the last time *Daily Cardinal* reporters attempted to use their media cards to cover a protest. "You just get beaten twice as hard," the reporter said. He wrote about his experience the next day.

"*Cardinal* reporter Leo Burt was beaten and had his gas mask confiscated by Dane County police who were not deterred by his press card."

To friends who visited with Burt a few days later, something had happened beyond the obvious physical wounds. Burt's head was bandaged to cover a gash in his forehead, his glasses held together by tape.

"Leo seemed different after the beating. He had been an armchair radical; now he was really pissed," said one acquaintance.

The revolution, for Leo Burt, was at hand.

"He was just shy of six feet, very muscular and vain about his physique, wearing tank tops to show off his well-developed pectorals," according to Tom Bates, author of *Rads: The 1970 Bombing of the Army Math Research Center at the University of Wisconsin and Its Aftermath.* "He had a drill sergeant's face, long and square-jawed and pitted with old acne scars. He had recently traded his horn rimmed glasses for a pair of wire rims and gotten rid of the Brylcream in his bathroom cabinet. He still wore heavy black hightops the Marines had issued him in his ROTC days and walked like Mr. Natural, the 'keep on truckin' hero of Zap Commix."

Leo Frederick Burt was born into a close-knit Catholic family on April 18, 1948, in Havertown, Pennsylvania, a Philadelphia suburb. By all accounts Burt was an unlikely candidate to do anything out of the ordinary. "He was usually quiet and reserved," according to Bates, "but loved to argue, the more esoteric the subject, the better. His speech came fast, with the big-city inflections of a Philadelphian. 'Yowza' he said when he agreed, and every other word was 'like.'"

Burt's generally reserved demeanor belied a more distinctive trait well-known to his friends: intensity. He pursued his interests obsessively. And Leo Burt's obsession during his formative years was rowing. Despite a less than ideal physique for

WANTED
BY THE FBI

SABOTAGE; DESTRUCTION OF GOVERNMENT PROPERTY; CONSPIRACY

LEO FREDERICK BURT

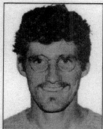  

Photograph taken in 1969   Photographic retouch

Alias: Eugene Donald Fieldston

DESCRIPTION

Dates of Birth Used:	April 18, 1948; April 15, 1950	**Hair:**	Brown (may now be gray)
Place of Birth:	Darby, Pennsylvania	**Eyes:**	Hazel
Height:	5'11" to 6'0"	**Sex:**	Male
Weight:	185 pounds	**Race:**	White
NCIC:	W735004020	**Nationality:**	American
Occupations:	Laborer and watchman		
Scars and Marks:	None known		
Remarks:	Burt may wear a moustache and beard and has worn his hair long in the back. He may also wear glasses. Burt has ties to New York City, New York; Boston, Massachusetts; and Peterborough, Ontario, Canada.		

CAUTION

Leo Frederick Burt is wanted for allegedly participating in the bombing of Sterling Hall, on the campus of the University of Wisconsin, on August 24, 1970. The blast from the explosion, combined with the fire, resulted in the death of a 33-year-old researcher. Additionally, there were several injuries reported and an estimated $6 million damage to the building and its contents. Reportedly, explosives had been placed in a stolen panel truck,

Leo Burt wanted poster

FEDERAL BUREAU OF INVESTIGATION

crew—considered short at five feet, eleven inches—he willed himself onto his high school and college teams and evangelized his obsession, openly dreaming of making the Olympics.

"Leo had infected his rowing mates with his passion for the sport, for the training and boat rigging, the science of it," Bates wrote. "In early spring when they were groaning from daily doubles, Leo would fire them up with glorious pictures of the rewards to come."

His mantra, repeated often to his colleagues: "An oarsman must be mentally tough."

Burt studied journalism at the UW and began writing sports stories for the *Cardinal*, which was saturated in the radicalism of the day. Eventually he was assigned to cover the Students for a Democratic Society organization, the burgeoning activist group on campus.

By his junior year Burt's intensity for rowing wasn't enough to compensate for his size. In a blow to dreams held since childhood, Burt was dropped from the traveling team on the eve of a national competition. He began acting out, voicing political views in the boathouse against club code, and challenging the mandatory haircut rule even though he wore his hair short.

"He still popped protein pills and worked out in the Old Red Gym," Bates wrote, "but the psychic energy that he had formerly put into rowing now went into reporting."

In the winter of 1970, as he was finishing his final semester of school, Burt quit the crew team, walking away from the one thing that had defined him since childhood. His intensity was now applied to the radicalism of the day. *Daily Cardinal* staff members were encouraged to join the militants: "Trash highly selective targets. Know your real enemies and do real damage. Do it first, then report it."

Burt initially opposed violence as a means of protest, then came the beating at the hands of police in May. The metamorphosis of Leo Burt—altar boy to crew mate to journalist to radical—was complete. Days later Burt joined an acquaintance in an attempt to firebomb the local draft board office. Their efforts failed when the ladder they used couldn't reach the second-floor office.

He was now part of the New Year's Gang. The self-titled "gang," in reality, was Karl Armstrong. On New Year's Eve 1970 Karl and his brother Dwight stole a small airplane (Dwight had taken a few, precious few, lessons) and flew to Sauk City north of Madison to drop Molotov cocktails on the Badger ammunition plant. Juggling bottles of kerosene with an open flame in the cockpit as the plane narrowly missed telephone lines in the dark, Karl dropped the bombs harmlessly into the snow near the plant, and even Karl admitted it was like a slapstick comedy routine. Nevertheless the New Year's Gang was born that night. Leo Burt, through his reporting at the *Cardinal*, was one of the few people who knew the identity of the gang. It was Karl whom Leo joined in the aborted firebombing of the draft board office in May. Armstrong then suggested the Army Math Research

Center in Sterling Hall as the gang's next target. Leo's response: "Yowza."

The Armstrong brothers and Burt took up residence in a downtown Madison apartment in the summer of 1970. In July Burt obtained an instructional pamphlet from the UW Extension on blasting with ANFO, an inexpensive mixture of ammonium nitrate and fuel oil commonly used by farmers to remove tree stumps. In August Burt convinced a fourth person, fellow *Cardinal* writer David Fine, to join the group.

The plan was to ignite a trailer packed with ANFO in the Sterling Hall loading dock on a summer night when school was out and the building would be empty.

With the proceeds from a marijuana deal, and merely guessing at the amount of ANFO to use, Armstrong and Burt bought forty-five gallons of fuel oil and 1,700 pounds of ammonium nitrate. Total cost: $56.12. Next they rented a trailer to carry the payload, but realizing they needed a large vehicle to pull the contents, Karl and Dwight had to stalk the UW campus until they found an unlocked van with the keys in the ignition.

One other thing the gang failed to consider: a contingency plan if the building appeared occupied, as it did at 3 a.m. on Monday, August 24, 1970.

"The place was lit up like a Christmas tree," according to Armstrong. He lit the five-minute fuse and ran to the nearest window. "And I spent, I would say, about ten or fifteen seconds at the window trying to make sure that there was no one in the building." Not seeing anyone inside, Armstrong and Burt sprinted to join their partners. Fine had made a warning call to the police from a nearby phone booth, and Dwight Armstrong drove the getaway car, a light-colored Corvair.

The blast resulted in the most destructive act of sabotage in United States history. (The 1994 Oklahoma City bombing, also caused by ANFO, now holds that infamous distinction.) The concussion lifted the gang's getaway car as they made their way down University Avenue. Minutes later the group stopped to marvel at the mushroom cloud rising over Madison.

The explosion woke people thirty miles away. Twenty-six campus buildings were damaged, including University Hospital. Scores of homes, businesses, and churches off campus were damaged. Inside Sterling Hall, which survived the blast, decades' worth of irreplaceable research in nuclear physics and superconductivity were obliterated. A major cancer study was gone. Army Math survived.

The group drove south to the community of Oregon, doubled back, and decided to spend the day at Devil's Lake State Park in Sauk County. Initial radio reports indicated no one had been injured in the blast. As dawn came the jubilant bombers were making their way to Devil's Lake when news broke that scientist Robert Fassnacht, whose lab was located on Sterling Hall's first floor, inside the window into which Armstrong had glanced, had been killed. The four revolutionaries were jolted into reality with the realization that they were now wanted for murder. Of the four, it was Burt who broke down in tears, muttering "Jesus fucking Christ" again and again.

A Madison patrolman had reported a light-colored Corvair speeding from campus when the bomb went off. Law enforcement across the upper Midwest was looking for the vehicle. As they approached Devil's Lake, a Sauk County sheriff's vehicle began tailing the students and within moments activated its lights. The four told the officers they were camping, though they had no camping gear, managing to explain calmly they were arriving early to vie for an open campsite and retrieving their gear later. The two officers believed they had the suspects in hand but Sauk County had nothing on which to hold them; they had broken no law in the county, and state law prohibited the detention of suspects without approval from the jurisdiction in which they were wanted. Unable to obtain a hold order from Dane County, which was in a state of utter chaos, the four were released by Sauk County after a couple of hours.

In the time the gang spent sweating it out in Sauk County, Dwight Armstrong noticed something about Leo Burt, the one person in the group who had taken the news of Fassnacht's death the hardest. Burt had grown silent, pensive, resolved. "He's cold as steel," Dwight thought. An oarsman must be mentally tough.

Returning to Madison after their narrow escape, and resigned to life underground, the four devised a hurried plan to escape to Canada via the East Coast. In a borrowed car they made their way to Michigan and Ohio, discovering along the way even the most militant of their underground colleagues wanted nothing to do with the New Year's Gang. They split up in Toledo. In New York Fine and Burt, the former *Cardinal* writers, wrote a media statement acknowledging the "unnecessary death" of Robert Fassnacht while justifying the bombing as a "necessary task." One week after the bombing Fine and Burt registered under assumed names in a Toronto area youth hostel.

Back in Madison an army of state and federal officers identified the suspects through the rented U-Haul trailer, the large quantities of fuel oil and fertilizer purchased nearby, and the Corvair registered to Karl Armstrong's father. The four men appeared on the FBI's Most Wanted list September 2, charged with sabotage, conspiracy, and destruction of government property. The State of Wisconsin would issue the murder charge separately.

The Royal Canadian Mounted Police, on high alert for the fugitives, identified Burt and Fine in the hostel. In his eagerness to close the net, FBI director J. Edgar Hoover personally announced that arrest warrants were being issued. But the federal charges (conspiracy, possession of explosives, and destruction of government property) were not extraditable. A new complaint had to be written. In the time it took to process new warrants, and thanks to Hoover's premature announcement, Fine and Burt had more than enough notice to flee. As Mounties waited in front of the hostel, the pair departed through a back window and went their separate ways. It was the last time Leo Burt's whereabouts were known.

Burt did not, however, vanish.

According to Bates, "Leo lived openly in another West Coast city, his whereabouts well known to the local heavies." He received financial support from sympathizers, and occasionally wrote apologias for the bombing that surfaced in radical publications.

The other three men were caught over the next seven years: Karl Armstrong in 1972, David Fine in 1976, and Dwight Armstrong in 1977. All three pled guilty, served jail terms, and resumed their lives.

Burt's final public letter appeared in the *Daily Cardinal* in March 1973. It urged support for Karl Armstrong, on trial in Madison, on the grounds that the entire student anti-war movement was being prosecuted with him. Burt's relatives and friends became jaded to the constant surveillance by authorities. Eventually the FBI became so frustrated in its manhunt that it began taking out ads in magazines, and even circulating Burt's acne prescription to pharmacies. But with the trail cold and the war ended, he was dropped from Most Wanted list in 1976.

The FBI kept at least one agent on the case, once sending Burt's fingerprints to every coroner and medical examiner in America to compare with John Does. Nothing. His parents' funerals were monitored, as was a 1989 reunion of Madison radicals. Nothing. In 1990 author Tom Bates theorized Burt was the Unabomber due to similarities in the manifestos written by Burt and, as it turned out, Ted Kaczynski, arrested in 1996.

Leo Burt became a punch line to folks in Wisconsin, a boogey man cited whenever strange or mysterious events occurred. Michael Zaleski, one of the prosecutors in the Karl Armstrong trial, noted Wisconsin has an official state bird, state animal and state insect. "Leo Burt ought to be our state ghost."

In 2007 another check of fingerprints against Burt's proved negative. A segment on *America's Most Wanted* television program produced more than one hundred tips but no results.

Some have speculated that Burt must have been a government infiltrator in the anti-war movement, receiving a new identity and protection following the bombing.

"He disappeared off the face of the Earth," said Zaleski. "You just don't do that. To me, there are only two plausible explanations: He's dead, or he was a plant by the government. That theory was floated for a while. Remember that Richard Nixon had his dirty tricks. Here's the reason I think that's minimally plausible: He was never found, and there was nothing in his background that would suggest that he was ever capable of this [crime].

"I think he's dead," Zaleski concluded. "I think that's the most plausible scenario."

In July 2010 as the fortieth anniversary of the Sterling Hall bombing approached, the FBI held a news conference to provide a briefing on the case. Leo Burt was still missing. The last fugitive from the '60s-era radicals would be nearly sixty years old. The FBI took the opportunity to reaffirm their efforts to apprehend Leo Frederick Burt.

"He needs to be accountable for what he did," said an agent in the Madison office. "He killed someone. Obviously there's a certain mystique in the early '70s. But the reality is that there was a young researcher doing nothing more than his job who lost his life.

"Until we've got credible information that he's no longer alive it remains a priority."

CHAPTER 12

Beerman: The Mobster Who Made Milwaukee Infamous

It was an early morning for Augie Palmisano, the owner of Palmy's Bar in Milwaukee. He had returned to his downtown apartment after closing time. Now, just a few hours later he was awake, dressed, and going back to work for the day, or at least part of the day. Palmisano paused a moment to stuff a batch of Summerfest tickets into his shirt pocket before locking the apartment door and walking downstairs to the parking garage.

It was 8:45 a.m., June 30, 1978, a cool and damp day. Palmisano entered his Mercury sedan, parked in its usual spot— stall number 33 of the Juneau Village apartments—and turned the key.

Folks living on Ogden and Juneau, North Milwaukee and Van Buren, the streets surrounding the apartments at 1319 North Jackson, recoiled from the sound of the blast. The heavy doors of the underground parking garage were bowed by the concussion, and thick black smoke billowed from the creases.

More than twenty vehicles inside the parking garage were destroyed or damaged by the explosion, the epicenter being a 1977 Mercury sedan parked in stall number 33.

Authorities identified the victim by his fingerprints. Oddly, his hands were left unscathed. The same could not be said for the rest of August S. Palmisano, forty-nine, owner of Palmy's Bar. Much of his flesh was blown off the bones. Police could only recognize fifteen charred Summerfest tickets in a shirt pocket.

An anonymous source, speaking to the *Milwaukee Journal* the day of Palmisano's demise, summed it up succinctly: "Augie opened his mouth."

Weeks after Palmisano's death, Frank Balistrieri, longtime head of the Milwaukee underworld and a man operating at the peak of his reign, hosted three out-of-town guests to clear up a misunder-standing. A vending machine business had started in Milwaukee and the upstarts were not aware Balistrieri received half of the profits.

The men were given a personal tour of the city in Balistrieri's enormous black Cadillac. They stopped at Festa Italiana, ate dinner at Frank's house, and drank seventy-dollar bottles of wine. They listened to the diminutive Balistrieri describe himself as the biggest man in Milwaukee. Later that night, when the group visited his de facto office in the corner of the Shorecrest Hotel restaurant to talk business, Balistrieri further impressed upon the group the scope of his power.

"Let me tell you what happened to a guy named Augie Palmisano," he began.

"He called me a name to my face," Balistrieri said, and then placing his fingers on his cheeks, shot a steely gaze at his guests and added, "now they can't find his skin."

It was said the only wrinkle he ever wore was a frown.

"He was small and slick, a man who hated the spotlight but always dressed as if he were ready for one," wrote one reporter who covered Balistrieri. The powerful head of the Milwaukee underworld for thirty years always maintained he was just a business owner and a family man. The FBI had a distinctly different opinion. Eventually they had the wiretaps to prove it.

Though decades have passed since its heyday, the dark mysteries of the Cream City Cosa Nostra linger. Surveillance and undercover work shed some light on the shadowy world of Frank Balistrieri, yet he escaped prosecution from the Feds' most serious charge: That he was the most dangerous man in Milwaukee, responsible for the violent deaths of at least a half-dozen people, as well as arson and bombings against those who defied him.

Thanks to geography, Milwaukee, best known for beer, sausages, and other Teutonic delights, could never attain the heights of larger mob centers. Located an hour or so up the road from Chicago, where they were writing the book on organized crime in the early half of the twentieth century, the brew city Mafia served its purpose as a satellite to the bosses residing across the state line. For all practical purposes Milwaukee was another neighborhood for the likes of Al Capone to corrupt as their own.

Milwaukee's place as Chicago's little sibling, underworld-wise, does not mean it was the weak sister. Not by a long shot. The Milwaukee Mafia began flexing its muscle early and often. As in other American cities, murders, bombings, and vice linked to the underworld began surfacing in the late 1890s.

Following a shooting death in Milwaukee's Italian neighborhood in 1898, authorities were unable to find a single person willing to speak on the matter. One resident, who chose to remain anonymous, told the *Milwaukee Sentinel*, "Of the 3,000 Italians residing in Milwaukee, ninety percent are from Sicily, and every Sicilian over 15 years of age may be classified as a member of the Mafia society."

Most of Milwaukee's close-knit Italian community had emigrated from Palermo, Sicily, as the anonymous source above pointed out. By and large they settled in the Third Ward on the lower near-east side, an area bounded by Michigan Street, Broadway, Lake Michigan, and the Milwaukee River.

By 1915 the Italian population had grown to more than six thousand residents, evidenced by twenty-nine Italian saloons, forty-five Italian groceries, an Italian bank, and two spaghetti factories. Produce warehouses, liquor distributors, dry goods businesses—capitalism was teeming in the Third Ward thanks to the entrepreneurial spirit of its denizens, a fact hardly lost to the underworld figures in their midst.

Vito Guardalabene had the distinction of being the first Milwaukee Mafia don imposed by the Chicago syndicate in 1918.

A succession of bosses followed. Peter Guardalabene (Vito's son), Joe Amato, Joe Vallone, Sam Ferrara, and John Alioto are generally accepted as having been the Milwaukee leaders until 1961.

In the meantime, in the 1930s, New Jersey underworld boss Lucky Luciano established a gangster board of directors dubbed the Commission to bring a degree of order to the underworld. The idea came from Sicily, where heads of different *cosche* (Mafia clans) would meet periodically to discuss business.

With a nod from the all-ruling Commission, Chicago maintained control of the region. The other city on Lake Michigan, the one known as Beer Town, never took a seat on the board. But it came close, thanks to the five-foot-six-inch Sicilian who called himself the biggest man in Milwaukee. To others he was Fancy Pants or Frankie Bal.

In a simple ledger book in Kansas City he was known, thanks to the reputation of his home city, as Beerman.

Frank Peter Balistrieri was born in Milwaukee in 1918, the son of Sicilian immigrants; his father was a trucker. Frank attended Lincoln High School and enrolled twice at Marquette University, never completing a degree. He was, nevertheless, articulate and refined, always dressed in a tailored suit; a talented musician with a penchant for the ladies.

"My idol was Al Capone as a kid," he once said. "That's a true story."

Admiration for Capone may have been a sign of things to come, but it was young love that opened the door for Balistrieri.

His childhood sweetheart Antonina Alioto was the daughter of John Alioto, the man who would become head of the Milwaukee underworld in the 1950s. Frank not only gained a wife with his marriage to Nina in 1939, but also became the trusted underling to his father-in-law and the boss-in-waiting. He was officially "made" a member of the Mafia, according to the FBI, in 1948.

Frank and Nina had four children: Joe, Bennedetta, John, and Catherine. During the early years Frank owned or controlled (as a hidden partner) various nightclubs, strip joints, and restaurants—La Scala, Leonardo's, Joey's Place, the Brass Rail, the Centre Stage, the Ad Lib, the Downtowner, Tradewinds, Gallagher's—and promoted boxing matches on the side.

The kids enjoyed a typical domestic upbringing under their mother's care while Dad brought home dinner guests such as bandleader Harry James and boxing great Rocky Marciano.

Wherever Frank trod, mysteries seemed to follow. One day in January 1960 the owner of the Brass Rail nightclub, Izzy Pogrob, disappeared without a trace. He was later found dead in a Mequon cornfield wearing a blindfold and seven bullet holes. (The three-hundred-pound Pogrob was frozen solid and had to be removed with a winch; it took days for the body to thaw.)

John Alioto retired in 1961, and it wasn't long before an FBI recording caught Frank describing to his father-in-law how he planned to handle two wayward Mafia soldiers.

"*L'amazzari.* I got to kill them."

By the end of the 1960s Balistrieri had been convicted of tax evasion and served two years in federal prison. The efforts of state and federal authorities to tie him to the most serious organized crime activities, however, were fruitless. Gambling, prostitution, extortion, illicit control of the produce industry, labor racketeering, and worse went unchecked.

The Marquette dropout had learned well.

Frank's next venture was beautiful in its simplicity. A southern California real estate developer named Allen Glick approached Balistrieri in the early '70s looking for a loan to purchase Las Vegas casinos. With hidden ownership of casinos and a seemingly legit front man in Glick, a man who knew when to look the other way, the Mafia began skimming casino profits like nobody's business. Every month tens of thousands of dollars in casino revenue were taken—before it could be tallied for tax purposes—and delivered by briefcase to Kansas City for distribution among Midwest mobsters. Frank Balistrieri made it happen. His labor connections secured a sixty-two-million-dollar loan from the corrupt Teamster Pension Fund to finance Glick's purchase of the Stardust and Fremont casinos.

Frank called the casino skim his monthly "transfusion." When some of the families started squabbling over the payments in 1975, a Kansas City mob comptroller was appointed to keep track of the loot. Between 1976 and 1979 more than two million dollars was skimmed. The comptroller stashed the ledgers in ventilation ducts in his house.

Back in Beer Town, business—Frank's kind of business—had never been better. His sons Joe and John, with law degrees from Notre Dame and Valparaiso, respectively, helped spread the wealth to avoid pesky IRS auditors. Most of Frank's assets were titled in his sons' names.

"You be diplomatic," he once directed his boys, "and I'll do the rough stuff."

Rough stuff like dealing with a "fink" named August Manciani, a skilled arsonist and burglar whom Frank suspected of talking to the FBI. On a golden June morning in 1975 Manciani returned to his modest Newhall Street house with the morning newspaper. As he stepped out of his car, Manciani was quietly shot five times in the head with a .22 caliber handgun equipped with a silencer.

"The scene was serene," wrote a reporter, "birds chirping, bloodstains were on the ground, the sun sparkled, the driver's door of the car was open and a copy of the *Milwaukee Sentinel* was on the ground, where Manciani had dropped it. He had become his own headline."

Unfortunately for the Manciani clan, August had a brother, Vincent, also connected. As he drove through Milwaukee one day, Vincent Manciani noticed his car was not performing properly. Opening the hood he saw the problem: Twenty sticks of dynamite wrapped around one pound of TNT. The bomb had failed to detonate due to a loose connection. Agents tailing Manciani asked who would have done such a thing.

"Kids," Manciani replied. He moved to Hawaii soon after.

Augie Palmisano, the owner of Palmy's Bar, was tight with the Manciani brothers. Augie's expressed unhappiness with the fate of the brothers made him a likely candidate to rat on Frank. Then Augie sealed his fate.

"He called me a name to my face . . . now they can't find his skin."

The comment sent chills through Frank's guests at Snug's restaurant in the Shorecrest Hotel, where the biggest man in Milwaukee conducted business at a table in the northwest corner. Two of his three guests that day in July 1978 were undercover agents, one from the Milwaukee FBI office, and another from New York who went by the name Donnie Brasco. The upstart Milwaukee vending machine business started by Brasco was bait in a federal sting.

The third member of Frank's party that night was New York hit man Benny "Lefty Guns" Ruggierio. Before their meeting with Frank, Lefty Guns prepped Brasco on Balistrieri: "He owns Kansas City. Cleveland and Detroit belong to Frank. This town, there's nothing you can do, you gotta go through him."

Frank was more to the point when he met his guests. "We've been looking for you all week. We were going to hit you."

Woven together with undercover agents, wiretaps, and mob informers, the net closed fast around Balistrieri. A raid on the Shorecrest Hotel turned up two hundred thousand dollars cash in plain brown envelopes. When Frank ignored the agents who appeared at his house with a search warrant they bashed in his front door with a sledgehammer, informing him that the "transfusions" were finished.

"He looked at me and realized that we knew about the skim," an agent reported. "I could see the confidence drain out of him. He knew it was over."

Frank and his sons faced a flurry of indictments starting in 1980. Joe and John were ultimately sentenced to eight years in prison for extortion. Frank was found guilty for his reign over gambling and extortion in Milwaukee, and he pled guilty in Kansas City to the Las Vegas skimming operation, receiving a total of thirteen years in federal prison.

He was released in 1991 and returned to his North Shepard Avenue home. During a visit to his daughter in California he toyed with the idea of writing a book. It must have been tempting for the compulsive braggart. At the same time, how could he ever reveal the truth without implicating himself? As one FBI agent noted before a Congressional committee, "We were seldom able to bring the cases to court due to an absence of cooperating or living witnesses, even though in almost every case we knew from informants who ordered the killings, as well as the identities of the mob members who actually carried out the crime."

The indictments of the 1980s knocked the teeth out of the mob in Milwaukee and elsewhere. Prison, old age, and occasionally more brutal methods perpetrated among its own, did the rest. The streets had changed too. Young, decidedly unorganized punks were the new gangsters in town. Law enforcement

Milwaukee underworld boss Frank Balistrieri, center, and two sons Joseph, left, and John, right, leave Kansas City, Missouri, Federal Court on Oct. 26, 1983, after entering a plea in the Las Vegas skimming case.

AP PHOTO/DOUG ATKINS

underwent a sea change to deal with the new crime wave. In Frank's heyday forty FBI agents were on his case in the Milwaukee office, but by the 1990s a lone agent was assigned to organized crime. The day of the don was dead.

Less than a year after their incarcerations began, in 1985, sons Joe and John did something remarkable. They talked. Against the Mafia's code of silence, the brothers appealed their prison terms by denouncing their father in lengthy letters to the court, stating they were "dragged kicking and screaming into this mess," insisting that they knew little of what their father was

MYTHS AND MYSTERIES OF WISCONSIN

doing, and characterizing him as an "evil force . . . inveterate liar and hopeless braggart."

Their bitter appeal succeeded. The sons were released after serving three years. Some speculated the boys were acting with their father's silent approval to gain early release, but it was a tone they maintained all the years following. "He had made our births a scandal," Joe said. The FBI evidence collected in the late 1970s seemed to back them up. "Brother John," Joe said at one point in a wiretapped conversation, "we had to do it his way and we were absolutely corrupted."

When John requested reinstatement to practice law in 1996, the vitriol flowed again, but the appeal was denied.

On Saturday night, February 6, 1993, Frank ate a heavy Italian dinner at a new restaurant in the lower east side, Joe and Mario's, 1601 North Jackson Street. The owners, thrilled with his visit, walked him to his car after dinner. He departed in his behemoth black Cadillac—nothing less would do for the biggest man in Milwaukee—to visit a female acquaintance living across the Milwaukee River. It was there, on a couch in an upstairs flat, that seventy-four-year-old Balistrieri died of a heart attack.

A private funeral mass was held at Old St. Mary's Church on North Broadway, just blocks from where he ate his last dinner, near the Juneau Village Apartments where the blast killed Augie Palmisano fifteen years earlier, not far from where Izzy Pogrob was last seen alive at the Brass Rail in January 1960, and less than a mile from the Third Ward neighborhood where

142

the Old World of Sicily and the New World of America inter-mingled a century earlier.

Two weeks before the funeral, the Milwaukee FBI unit had moved into new offices located across the street from Old St. Mary's Church. Fittingly in death as in life, Frank Balistrieri went under the watchful eyes of federal agents.

Family matriarch Nina died in 1997. The couple is buried in Milwaukee's Holy Cross Cemetery. Following their release from prison, sons Joe and John lived quietly in the Shorecrest Hotel, ever protective of their privacy. Joe died of natural causes in 2010 at age seventy.

CHAPTER 13

The Myth of the Marinette Mercenary

On Sunday morning, October 5, 1986, a C-123 supply plane, a Vietnam-era military aircraft with a 360-foot wingspan, departed San Salvador, El Salvador, heading south over the Pacific Ocean. Turning 180 degrees to enter Costa Rican airspace near the northwest corner of the country, the plane failed to report its position, as it was required to do, before continuing north toward Nicaragua. The plane, capable of holding as many as sixty soldiers, contained a crew of four civilians. Its payload: thirteen thousand pounds of cargo carefully prepared for air-drop.

Twenty miles north of San Carlos, Nicaragua, two teenage soldiers sat quietly in the Central American rain forest armed with two deadly weapons: a surface-to-air rocket launcher, and dreams of blowing one of those enormous planes out of the sky.

Just after noon the drone of the aircraft lumbering a thousand feet above the jungle to avoid radar detection came into earshot. Nineteen-year-old Jose Fernando Canales and his comrade-in-arms scrambled into position. Canales balanced the rocket launcher on his shoulder, pointing it skyward toward the flight path taken by previous supply planes. Through the trees the pair could see the plane's cargo hold gaping open underneath the tail section in preparation for the drop. His pulse racing, the young soldier aimed the weapon through a clearing in the trees and pulled the trigger. He wasn't concerned about accuracy—the heat seeking missile would take care of that.

The rocket emerged from the jungle, hesitating for a split second as it locked onto the aircraft's exhaust plume, then shot toward its mark. The starboard wing was blown to pieces and the aircraft spun into the jungle. As the two soldiers celebrated their kill, they noticed something drifting away from the smoky trails leading down to the horizon: a parachute.

It took a day for Nicaraguan soldiers to make their way through the jungle. The wreckage yielded everything they had hoped for and more: 50,000 ammunition cartridges, 70 assault rifles, 60 grenade launchers, 150 pairs of jungle boots, and— scattered among the remains of three dead crew members— detailed flight records, identification badges, and notebooks full of contact names. The cache of intelligence was more valuable than the payload itself.

There remained the prospect of a potential survivor, the lone parachutist seen drifting from the aircraft. The Nicaraguan government knew that apprehending a crew member, in addition to the evidence discovered at the crash site, would be a prize beyond their wildest hopes.

A day later soldiers surrounded an abandoned jungle shack near the crash zone. Lying inside in a hammock made from his parachute was a strapping red-headed American eating a squash.

"Give it up, gringo, or we'll blow you to hell."

The gringo gave it up.

The American was "nervous, completely demoralized, frightened," according to one of the soldiers. "He knew he was doing something wrong in someone else's country."

Marched to a base camp, the disheveled and disheartened American was photographed being led from the jungle with a rope tied around his wrists. Jose Fernando Canales had the honors. The next day the prisoner was flown by helicopter to Managua, where a soldier greeted him by patting him on the shoulder and laughing, "So what now, Rambo?"

Nicaraguan officials hastily assembled the international media for a photo opportunity. The prisoner was whisked into a room teeming with reporters from around the globe. No questions were allowed, no introductions were made, no *we told you so* speeches by the government officials—just a spark to ignite an international firestorm delivered by a man who had been an unemployed construction worker months earlier:

"My name is Gene Hasenfus. I come from Marinette, Wisconsin. I was captured yesterday in southern Nicaragua. Thank you."

A man identified as Eugene Hasenfus, center, is led to a helicopter by Sandinista soldiers in El Tule, Nicaragua, after his plane was downed by Sandinista forces, Oct. 7, 1986.

The incident was the ultimate triumph for Nicaraguan President Daniel Ortega and his Sandinista National Liberation Front government. After years of charging the United States with perpetrating an illegal war against the country and its Marxist government, the proof appeared scattered across the jungle floor north of San Carlos and embodied in what Nicaraguan radio described as the "tall, blond, and strong" American, "just like one always imagined a pure gringo would be."

It was an era when the Cold War was simmering hot. Upon taking office in 1981, US President Ronald Reagan charged Ortega's Sandinistas of "exporting revolution" to other Central American nations, namely El Salvador, and authorized the Central Intelligence Agency (CIA) to begin financing, arming, and training anti-communist guerrillas known as Contras. In 1984 it was discovered that Nicaraguan harbors had been mined in clear violation of international law. It was also apparent the Contras were incapable of executing such an operation. Indeed the mines had been procured and shipped by the CIA, then planted in the harbors by CIA-trained commando teams using high-speed boats.

Fearing the United States was becoming immersed in another Vietnam, Congress cut off military aid to the Contras in the fall of 1984. It was a major setback for the Reagan administration, which was promoting the Contras as "freedom fighters" and the "moral equivalents of America's founding fathers."

The prohibition on government military assistance resulted in a shift to private mercenaries funded by sympathetic nations around the world, according to the White House. Others begged to differ. "I've had it up to here with Nicaragua and the way the Administration uses the CIA to run its paramilitary operations," seethed one senator. Another senator characterized the CIA operations as evidence of Reagan's "wink and shrug" foreign policy.

In the spirit of this deeply murky arrangement, Eugene Hasenfus, forty-five, received a call from an old Marine buddy named Bill Cooper. The call could not have come at a better time for Hasenfus, unemployed with three young children in 1986. He had worked construction and odd jobs for more than decade, including a stint as a sky-diving instructor with his brother, but times were tough for a working man in Marinette and its cross-river neighbor of Menominee, Michigan, an area jokingly referred to as the "Twin Cities" by residents.

Hasenfus was a local boy. He played football for Marinette High School, including the big rivalry game against Menominee in the fall of 1959, and like any North Woods denizen, Gene loved hunting and fishing and watching the Green Bay Packers with his beer drinking buddies down at the Boom County Saloon. Following high school Hasenfus entered the Marines. Honorably discharged after five years, his post-Marine career proved most fateful. In the mid-sixties Gene, along with pilot Cooper, began working for Air America, a corporation run by the CIA for covert operations in Indochina. Hasenfus was a loadmaster, "a kicker," the guy who readies cargo for airdrop, a perfect job for a working man. And the pay was very good.

With the end of US involvement in Vietnam, Gene returned to Wisconsin to make a living and raise a family with his wife, Sally.

Cooper's phone call to his old friend in June 1986 was more than social. He needed a kicker for the C-123s working in Central America, and he knew just the man for the job. To Hasenfus it didn't really matter by whom or how this thing was organized—though he was sympathetic toward the policy of aiding the Contras— the particulars were incidental to taking a job he could do well and that paid three thousand dollars a month. It would be just like 'Nam. Instead of Air America he would be working for something called Corporate Air Services, which, like the former, looked a hell of a lot like the CIA. Should anything happen, Gene told his wife, contact the highest levels of the government.

In fact, Corporate Air had a policy identical to the CIA: No parachutes for employees flying missions. Why? Dead men can't talk. A parachute just might save somebody's life and deliver him into unfriendly hands. Hasenfus ignored the rule and borrowed his brother's parachute when he left for Central America.

Arriving in El Salvador in July 1986, Hasenfus reported to Felix Rodriguez, aka Max Gomez. Rodriguez was a CIA saboteur inside Cuba during the ill-fated Bay of Pigs campaign, and he played a key role in the capture and execution of Latin American revolutionary Che Guevara. As Max Gomez he was no longer a CIA employee, but like everything else, it was hard to tell the difference.

Sally had precious little information on her husband's job other than his advice to contact the highest levels of the government if anything happened. She did just that when Gene's brief statement in Managua was blasted worldwide by the news media, calling the State Department in a state of shock, saying her husband was the guy on TV and he "works for the CIA."

"For a while Tuesday, it seemed that every news gathering organization in the free world had a rabid interest in Marinette," reported the local *Eagle-Star* newspaper.

Not only that, it seemed every news organization in the free world was camped on Sally Hasenfus's front lawn. While Sally worked feverishly to find out what was going on, William Hasenfus told the Associated Press that his brother "was the type of guy who goes looking for trouble," an off-the-cuff comment the family would come to regret.

US officials from the President on down insisted that the government had nothing to do with Hasenfus or the supply missions.

"We've been aware that there are private groups and private citizens that have been trying to help the Contras," Reagan said in a news conference, "but we did not know the exact particulars of what they were doing."

Hasenfus told his captors he had participated in ten supply flights, and that the flights had been coordinated by men who worked for the CIA, a claim countered immediately by the US Assistant Secretary of State: "This was not a US government operation. It was not US financed. It was not CIA."

On October 11, five days after Hasenfus was captured, Mike Wallace of CBS's *60 Minutes*, along with a television crew, appeared in the Managua prison to interview Gene. Broadcast to twenty million homes, the interview revealed nothing other than to show the prisoner was hesitant to say anything of substance; he had been denied the opportunity to speak to counsel since his capture.

The State Department lent its assistance to unite Sally and Gene—he was, after all, a US citizen stranded in a foreign land—but the government was only going so far. Since Gene was technically an employee of a private company, Corporate Air Services, and not the government, all expenses, including travel and the imminent legal bills for Gene's defense, would be incurred by the family.

"I'm scared because he's a political orphan out there," brother William Hasenfus said, "and nobody's owning up to who he worked for or what."

Meanwhile, the Nicaraguan government announced it would put Hasenfus on trial for violating "the maintenance of order and public security." He faced thirty years in prison. The court, known as the People's Tribunal, had a conviction rate of 99.8 percent.

Former US Attorney General Griffin Bell, practicing law in Atlanta, was hired by the Hasenfus family to represent Gene, but the Nicaraguan government refused to allow any American other than Sally (and Mike Wallace) to speak to Hasenfus. A Nicaraguan defense attorney who feared for his life was hired to represent the defendant.

Sally Hasenfus pleaded for moral and financial support from the public. A petition asking for Hasenfus's release was posted at the Pine Tree Mall in Marinette, and an account was established for monetary donations.

In late October the *Marinette Eagle-Star* weighed in with an editorial:

We sympathize with the family and friends of Eugene Hasenfus at what is undoubtedly the most difficult time in their lives. However, as the situation now stands, we question the naiveté of those people who insist that Hasenfus be freed.

Whether Hasenfus worked for the CIA or not, there seems to be little dispute that he was doing something that he should not have been.

We wonder how this country would react if the situation was reversed. It is doubtful that we would release a "terrorist" and send him on his way with only a slap on the wrist just because his home country demanded it.

The Hasenfus family's attorney in Marinette spoke to the challenges facing the clan: "The comment you hear frequently is, 'He got himself into it, it's his own problem, or the government got him into it, the government will get him out of it.'"

The trial, begun late October 1986, was, predictably, a circus. The Nicaraguan government introduced a lengthy diatribe detailing a century of "Yankee interventionism."

"He is an absolute pawn, that's what the trial is about," said an outraged Bell as he left Nicaragua never having been able to consult with his client.

Meanwhile, two other events were indirectly conspiring against Hasenfus. For one, Congress approved the Reagan administration's one hundred-million-dollar request to jumpstart the military aid to the Contras, which had been banned since 1984. The approval instantly rendered private military operations obsolete. In practical terms this meant the problems of some guy captured at the eleventh hour before US military aid started flowing again became an afterthought. A government official told the Associated Press the private operations were "amateurish" and "poorly conceived," pointing to Hasenfus as an example: He "seemed not to know what to do with himself other than to hang around and wait until he was captured."

The second thing working against Hasenfus originated halfway around the world, in Lebanon, where a newspaper revealed the United States had been selling arms to Iran in exchange for the release of American hostages being held by terrorists, a direct contradiction of US policy. The sensational arms-for-hostages scheme rapidly mushroomed into the biggest political scandal since Watergate as further revelations showed profits from the arms sales had been diverted illegally to the Contras. The scandal and the subsequent investigations would command the nation's attention for a year.

The reality emerging from this geopolitical maelstrom: Gene Hasenfus was becoming a footnote to history nearly as quickly as he had become a worldwide figure. He was, as his brother put it, a "political orphan," ignored by his government, abandoned by his employer, exploited by his captors, and obscured by larger events.

On November 15, Hasenfus was convicted and sentenced to thirty years in prison. In a span of weeks the simple working man from Marinette had been shot out of the sky (which killed his friend Bill Cooper and two others), captured in a jungle, paraded in front of the world media, jailed in a dingy Nicaraguan cell, interviewed by Mike Wallace of *60 Minutes*, put on trial in a kangaroo court, and sentenced to three decades' imprisonment. A court appeal was thrown out. The only hope remaining was for the Sandinista government, having wrung every bit of propaganda out of his capture, to pardon Hasenfus.

"In the beginning, he would ask about other things, like how the Packers are doing," reported Sally, who made numerous trips to support her husband.

The emotional roller coaster took off again December 17 when Hasenfus was told suddenly he had been pardoned as a gesture of peace. He spent the night at the US Embassy and arrived in Green Bay the next evening for an emotional reunion with his children. The next day the family visited a Christmas tree farm, a media contingent following close at hand. A party was held later at the Boom County Saloon. Hasenfus laughed when his high school football coach mentioned that he had pledged fifty dollars a month until Gene was free, which would have cost eighteen thousand dollars had the full sentenced been served.

"I'm just glad he didn't have to pay it," Hasenfus said.

The matter of expenses loomed large. The relief fund had raised $5,600, a fraction of the debt facing the family.

In 1990 Eugene and Sally sued Corporate Air Services. The couple sought compensation for the huge legal and travel bills amassed, maintaining they were assured throughout the ordeal that the costs would be covered. The civil suit was discounted by attorneys for Corporate Air, who said Hasenfus knew the risks associated with the flights.

Four years removed from the incident and the strain was taking a toll. Gene told reporters he hoped the suit would finally help "put all this far behind me. I just want to forget about this, pretend it never happened." Sally said if she didn't have three kids, "I would have fled and started a new life."

The Federal Court in Miami dismissed the couple's suit. An appeal two years later was dropped. As a last resort a Wisconsin congressman drafted legislation to compensate the Hasenfus family from the US Treasury. The proposal never made it out of committee.

The ensuing years were not kind to Eugene Hasenfus. Book and movie deals never materialized. Compensation for expenses and damages never came. The only thing to show for it all was a mountain of debt and a nasty case of post-traumatic stress. Sally, who worked tirelessly on her husband's behalf during his captivity, couldn't bear the endless strain on their marriage, divorcing Gene in 1998. His life became a string of financial and legal woes, including arrests for battery/obstruction of a police officer, taking equipment from an employer, illegally hunting and killing a bear, and indecent exposure, an act he described as "one of the most ignorant, stupid, most embarrassing things that has ever happened to me."

In the late '90s Hasenfus found a job as an ironworker on the construction of Miller Park, the Milwaukee Brewers' new stadium. He told a reporter he didn't care much for talking about himself or "the Gene Hasenfus story—none of that shit." Instead he heaped praise on his fellow ironworkers. "They're busting their rear ends, they're some of the best." He talked about the intricacies of the stadium project. "This job is an adventure right here." And the man from Marinette who was called a mercenary, gun runner, and soldier of fortune a thousand times over from one corner of the globe to the other offered perhaps the best insight of who he was and how he ended up on the world's stage the fall of 1986.

"There's nothing wrong with hard work. I don't think any decent American is afraid of hard work. That's what it's all about.

"I'm trying to make a living and that's it."

CHAPTER 14

The La Crosse Serial Killer

On Thursday afternoon, April 15, 2004, the police chief of La Crosse, Wisconsin, the scenic college town located along the Mississippi River valley, stood at a podium in the city's public safety building, grim and determined. Less than twenty-four hours earlier authorities had recovered the body of University of Wisconsin-La Crosse student Jared Dion in the Mississippi near Riverside Park downtown.

That a person had drowned in the deep, treacherous, and typically frigid river was not necessarily newsworthy of a press conference. But Dion was the seventh person to die under identical circumstances in a seven-year span. In that time various websites ignited fears that too many similarities existed for the deaths to be coincidental. One website expanded the scope of the theory to include a total of fifteen deaths in the Upper Midwest.

Police Chief Ed Kondracki called the news conference to announce the findings of the investigation into Dion's death, but

College town La Crosse, Wis., is home to the world's largest six-pack.

MICHAEL BIE PHOTO

the obvious intent was to end rampant talk consuming La Crosse that a serial killer was stalking local college students—virtually the only topic being discussed in the city from the moment Dion was announced missing Sunday morning. When the twenty-one-year-old's body was discovered days later, it confirmed what countless people just knew to be true. *These can't all be accidents.*

There was no killer in La Crosse, officials believed. Dion's blood alcohol content, Kondracki announced at the news conference, was 0.27, more than three times the legal limit.

"There is no evidence of foul play," the chief said firmly. "No evidence of any kind of altercation. No sign of a fight that took place. We found no evidence that Jared was being stalked. We found no one who had resentment toward him, was angry with him or anything like that. There was just no evidence he had any contact with anyone after he was last seen."

The police concluded Dion had accidentally fallen into the river. He left his friends near a downtown bar about 2:30 a.m., purportedly to catch a bus. Why he walked two blocks west to the riverfront was a mystery.

"It's hard for most anyone to know" what a person is thinking with that level of intoxication, Kondracki responded.

"The common denominators in these past cases are excessive intoxication coupled with individuals venturing out onto or falling into the Mississippi, where the water is extremely deep and the current very fast," Kondracki said. "I am absolutely convinced that no crimes have been committed and these cases are extremely unfortunate mishaps."

The police findings were assailed. City officials received nonstop phone calls and e-mails. The *La Crosse Tribune* and the Internet were inundated with angry comments refuting the investigation; the newspaper began devoting its editorial pages to run a fraction of the letters. National media swarmed to report on the scenic but troubled river community.

"I would like to know why it is so far out of the realm of possibility . . . to acknowledge that we have a very odd series of events take place and that these deaths could very well be linked in some way?" one resident asked.

"We don't know if there is a serial killer in our neighborhood, but it seems a distinct possibility," another said. "Please do not say again that no foul play is suspected and leave it at that. Something is going wrong here."

"Well, I don't buy it!" a resident wrote in the *Tribune*. "Seven male bodies aged 18 to 24 have been found in the river during the past seven years. It is far too many 'tragic accidents' to be occurring in such a short time span."

The arguments for foul play pointed to the number of commonalities: The victims were all white males between the ages of seventeen and twenty-seven, college students or recent graduates, and high achievers or student athletes in good physical condition. They were last seen drinking with friends and vanished between 10 p.m. and 4 a.m., and between September and April.

Police chief Kondracki moved quickly to shift the debate to alcohol awareness and beefing up riverside safety measures. In a letter to Mayor John Medinger he suggested the city "seriously consider installing an attractive gate or similar barrier" along the riverfront.

The letter received a tepid reply.

"I don't want a knee-jerk response, but I want a thoughtful response," Medinger told the *La Crosse Tribune*. "Many of the things the chief suggested sound reasonable, but we're not going to fence off the Mississippi River. We don't have the money, and I don't think it would accomplish anything."

Kondracki shot back: "I'm not talking about putting up a fence from Minneapolis to New Orleans. I'm just talking about a fence along Riverside Park. That doesn't seem like anything that would be too costly."

In an interview with the *Milwaukee Journal Sentinel*, Wisconsin's most widely read newspaper, Medinger expanded his comments.

"Do I think there is a serial killer out there? No. Am I absolutely sure? No. Who can be? Most people here do believe that there is something going on."

The issue had caused a "disconnect" between the community and the police, Medinger told the newspaper, and the city needed to find a way to help the public understand the evidence in the case.

Then he added, "My wife thinks it's a serial killer. She's totally convinced."

Kondracki went ballistic.

"Our officers consider themselves part of the community they serve, not removed from the community they serve." As far as the mayor's wife, Kondracki told the *Tribune*, "He says she is totally convinced, yet she has never asked to see the police reports. She has never talked to me. She has never talked to Captain Brohmer. And, she has never talked to DCI [Division of Criminal Investigation]. It makes me wonder what she bases her conclusions on."

On the UW-La Crosse campus, Kim Vogt, chairwoman of the sociology department and an instructor of criminology, along with Betsy Morgan, the head of the psychology department, began working on a response to the serial killer mania gripping the campus. Over the years Vogt had been asked routinely about the river deaths in her criminology classes. Vogt and Morgan's collaboration resulted in an open letter that university officials distributed immediately to every student's e-mail account.

"Throughout your college careers, you will be asked to engage in critical thinking," the letter began. "Nowhere is critical thinking more important than when you apply your education and training to your own lives and experiences."

The letter noted the leading cause of death among young men is unintentional accidents, and young males are ten times more likely to suffer accidental drowning than young women. But the letter's harsh truth was gleaned from UW-L's own student population. A survey showed that 30 to 40 percent of the 3,559 male students on campus were binge drinkers.

"Therefore, on any given Friday night in downtown La Crosse there may be up to 1,140 very drunk 18–24-year-old male UW-L students downtown. Even if the number of male UW-L students downtown was one-tenth of this estimate, there would be 114 drunken UW-L males downtown. Many may wander about after the bars close, some will wander toward the river. Every now and then, someone will fall in and drown." The survey did not include the student population of two other colleges located in La Crosse.

"Perhaps even more of a concern is that it is somehow more comforting for us to think that Jared's death was caused by something we cannot control (e.g., a serial killer) rather than a cause we can control (not getting drunk, always keeping an eye on your buddies to ensure their safe return home). It is often harder to accept explanations that hit close to home—explanations that involve actions we ourselves have engaged in that put us at risk."

One week had passed since Dion's body was recovered. It seemed not a dent had been made in calming the serial-killer hysteria despite the best efforts of authorities. The besieged police chief called a public meeting at La Crosse Central High School. A crowd of 1,500 packed the auditorium for the meeting, which was broadcast live by local television and radio.

A panel of police and university and health officials reviewed the cases, including blood alcohol content, autopsy findings, and the official cause of death. The tension was palpable. As the panel attempted to dispel the arguments made for foul play the meeting descended into open hostility. Skeptics began shouting down the panelists. Audience members tore into the official findings and were cheered enthusiastically.

Kim Dion, mother of the most recent victim, confronted the panel from her seat in the auditorium.

"That was my son and I have a right to believe any story I hear and to pursue that," she yelled as the audience applauded. Outside the hall she told reporters another person must have been with her son. "I don't believe Jared was down by the river by himself. It makes no sense for him to be there. It's not somewhere he would go."

Dan Marcou, a La Crosse police lieutenant and an uncle of one of the drowning victims, fought back tears as he admonished the crowd.

"My family has to be dragged through this over and over again every time there's another drowning. The La Crosse police department investigated all of these thoroughly. Then we have to listen to people applaud at the thought that my nephew was killed by a serial killer. This community is like an alcoholic. It would rather think a killer is loose than admit that it's got a drinking problem."

The skeptics pressed on relentlessly despite Marcou's testimony. *Why would these deaths just start happening now?* They didn't, the panel responded. Six college-aged men drowned in the local rivers from 1974 to 1979, and eight more drowned between 1980 and 1989. *Why doesn't this happen on other campuses?* It does, but it's worse here because the river is eighteen feet deep at the edge with a strong current. *What about all the similarities among the victims?* On any given weekend in downtown La Crosse there are hundreds if not thousands of people who fit the profile: college-aged males, mostly Caucasian, many of them drink, and when they do it's between the hours of 10 p.m. and 4 a.m. between the months of September and April when school is session. Another theory says the serial killer stalks high achievers and students in good physical condition; a serial killer couldn't possibly know this. *Why doesn't this happen to females?* Women are socialized to stay together; they're less likely to wander off alone. *Why would they go to the river?* It's not hard to imagine; he's drunk, maybe depressed, thinks that walking in the fresh air will clear his head. He feels nauseous and leans over the water to vomit, or decides to splash his face, or stumbles and slips.

The panel's responses, if they were able to respond at all before being drowned out by choruses of boos, were inadequate against the withering emotional assaults coming from the angry crowd. *The police were incompetent, Keystone cops, oblivious to clues in front of their noses.*

One person suggested the serial killer could be a member of the police force.

Kondracki received a sarcastic round of applause when he said the state Division of Criminal Investigation was conducting an independent review. (The division, in fact, had essentially completed its review and supported the police department's findings.)

After nearly two hours of unbridled hostility, Kondracki called for a brainstorming session to discuss safety precautions. About a third of the audience walked out; those who remained angrily demanded answers to their questions about a serial killer, often dwelling on the details of police reports, such as the location of Dion's baseball hat found in Riverside Park.

The panel members were left shell-shocked by the meeting.

"If I had the town hall meeting to do again this close to an accident like that," Dr. Christine Miller told the newspaper, "I would have just had it to listen, listen, listen. In my experience if I had a patient in that much pain, and the community is in that much pain—I would just listen. At that point and time, I would not give facts." Miller said she was surprised by the anger. "I didn't realize how much people needed to vent. I was also surprised people didn't realize we have to do this together."

Mayor Medinger, who was unable to attend due to a speaking commitment in Iowa, listened to most of the meeting on the radio. He echoed Dr. Miller's sentiments and tweaked Chief Kondracki, telling the *Tribune,* "There was too much talk and not enough listening."

For all its bucolic scenes—majestic bluffs standing shoulder to shoulder over the river valley, tree-lined streets, and alleys shading distinctive Victorian homes—La Crosse has never been the model of temperance. At its heart La Crosse is a river city, spawned by the likes of people who made the town the wild west before there was a Wild West. Decades later, in the war years of the 1940s, the city's reputation re-emerged as soldiers from Camp McCoy—GIs who wondered if they might soon be fighting and dying on a distant shore—poured into La Crosse on weekend leave.

In 1961 the city began its famous Oktoberfest celebration (an idea conceived by workers in the hometown G. Heileman Brewery) and five years later experienced its first, and definitely not its last, drunken riot. Annually through the '70s and '80s hundreds of arrests were made during festival weekend—there could have been thousands, according to the police—and riots were common. In the early 1990s, following an annual student bacchanal known as the Coon Creek Canoe Races, fire hoses and tear gas had to be used to disperse violent, drunken mobs.

In 1993 the police department began developing strategies to reduce confrontation, virtually eliminating large-scale problems during Oktoberfest and throughout the year. But getting a handle on the city's culture of drinking was like squeezing a balloon: Problems associated with the longstanding tradition of good times in La Crosse simply emerged elsewhere, just as sure as the world's largest six-pack stands on Third Street.

On a Friday night during Oktoberfest 2006, Luke Homen, a twenty-one-year-old UW-La Crosse student athlete from Brookfield, Wisconsin, spent the night barhopping downtown. In the haze of the evening, as thousands of people poured onto the streets at closing time, Homen vanished. His friends never knew the gregarious Homen to behave that way. They reported him missing the next day.

"None of it makes any sense," one of Homen's basketball teammates said. "There's a four-hour time span where none of our friends, none of his friends, nobody, knows where he was."

Homen's body was discovered in the water near Riverside Park two days later, the eighth victim in nine years. His blood alcohol content was 0.32.

Though not as acute as two years earlier, the stubborn rumors of a serial killer were enough to compel La Crosse police to ask the FBI to review the cases. Once again chief Kondracki called a news conference to tout the findings. The FBI's National Center for Analysis of Violent Crime found no evidence to support the serial killer theory and there were no connections found between the deaths. According to the FBI report, eight people who accidentally fell into the water and survived reported no contact with anyone else, nor were there any reports of a suspicious person approaching men in the area. Just as illuminating, if not simply frightening, the report noted that a total of forty drunk people had been stopped at the water's edge by student volunteers who had been patrolling the area since Dion's death in 2004.

The report went far in extinguishing lingering talk of a serial killer. The news conference did provide a kernel of suspicion for conspiracy theorists inhabiting the Internet: Kondracki refused to release a copy of the report, saying it was FBI property.

On a Saturday night in February 2010, Craig Meyers, a twenty-one-year-old Western Technical College student, attended a wedding reception held at a La Crosse bowling alley before hitting the bars downtown. Meyers's cousin offered to give him a ride at closing time. Meyers asked to be dropped off on the 700 block of Market Street, stating he was near his girlfriend's house even though she lived at least nine blocks to the east.

He was reported missing the next day. For the ninth time in recent memory the sight of crews dragging the river appeared near Riverside Park, friends of the missing person gathered to pray for an improbable happy ending, and utter disbelief reigned that this was happening all over again. Meyers's body was recovered from the Mississippi two days later. He had died of cold water drowning with acute alcohol intoxication and hypothermia as contributing factors. There were no signs of trauma to the body.

But one thing was noticeably lacking in the sad aftermath: fears of a sociopath killing college students. A surveillance camera owned by a downtown business captured the image of Meyers walking west, alone, about 2 a.m. A bloodhound tracked his scent to the river. There, a single set of footprints in the snow led to an open spot in the ice twenty feet offshore.

Approximately a week after Meyers's death in February 2010, as the bars were emptying in downtown La Crosse following a typically boozy Saturday night, no less than four drunken individuals—males, white, young, by all appearances healthy—were halted as they approached the river. Of the four, two were lost and thought they were walking east rather than west. One was trying to find a nearby hotel. The fourth refused to show his ID and became belligerent with the police.

"Where are you headed?" an officer asked.

"To the river."

BIBLIOGRAPHY

CHAPTER 1, HOLY(?) APPARITIONS

"Final Visit of the Blessed Virgin Reported Saturday," *Necedah Republican,* October 12, 1950.

McCann, Dennis, "Visits drew crowds, not credence," *Milwaukee Journal Sentinel,* April 2, 1998.

Morrell, Alex, "Virgin Mary apparitions near Green Bay shrine recognized as first in U.S." *Green Bay Press Gazette,* December 9, 2010.

———, "Faithful pouring into Marian shrine," *Green Bay Press Gazette,* July 6, 2011.

"Mrs. Van Hoof Awaits Vision," *La Crosse Tribune,* August 13, 1950.

"Mrs. Van Hoof Quotes Words Spoken Again," *La Crosse Tribune,* August 16, 1950.

"Pilgrims Gather at Necedah Shrine," *Necedah Republican,* August 17, 1950.

Queen of the Holy Rosary Mediatrix of Peace Shrine, www .necedahshrine.com.

Shrine of Our Lady of Good Help, www
.shrineofourladyofgoodhelp.com.

Sly, Randy, "Wisconsin Shrine Approved as First U.S. Marian
Apparition Site," Catholic Online, December 12, 2010.

"Special Pilgrimage Trains to Necedah," *Necedah Republican,*
August 10, 1950.

CHAPTER 2, WAUKAUKAUMMAHAUT: SON OF THE SOUTHERN
PRESIDENT

"Jeff Davis' Wisconsin Elopement Which Really Wasn't an
Elopement," *Milwaukee Journal,* February 24, 1928.

"Jefferson Davis in the '30s," *Milwaukee Sentinel,* November
10, 1895.

"Jefferson Davis Met and Won Daughter of Zachary Taylor
At Fort Crawford," *Wisconsin State Journal,* November 25,
1923.

Menominee Civil War Veterans, Wisconsin Veterans Resource
Center, 1994. OCLC: 54777513.

Menominee Tribal Historic Preservation Department,
*Menominee Veterans, A Photo History of Our Land, Our
Battles, Our Victories,* August 2010.

"Overview of Menominee History," Menominee Tribal Historic
Preservation Department, www.menominee-nsn.gov.

"Sarah Knox Taylor Davis," The Papers of Jefferson Davis, Rice University, http://jeffersondavis.rice.edu

Zachary Taylor, White House, www.whitehouse.gov.

CHAPTER 3, THE LOST PRINCE

Bonaparte, Darren, "The Unquiet Rest of Eleazor Williams," *The People's Voice,* May 6, 2005.

"Death of the Rev. Eleazor Williams, the Pretended Dauphin of France," *New York Times,* September 4, 1858.

Holmes, Fred, "Royalty Beckons a Creole," *Badger Saints and Sinners,* E.M. Hale and Company, Copyright 1939.

Srubas, Paul, "DNA debunks Lost Dauphin tale," *Green Bay Press Gazette,* April 20, 2000.

Swardson, Anne, "A Telltale Heart Finds Its Place in History," *Washington Post Foreign Service,* April 20, 2000.

CHAPTER 4, A CAPITOL OFFENSE

Bruce, William George, and Josiah Seymour Curry, *History of Milwaukee Vol. 1,* Milwaukee-Chicago: S.J. Clarke Publishing, 1922, 91.

"Founding Father Byron Kilbourn returns to Milwaukee," Historic Milwaukee, Inc., Resources, www.historicmilwaukee .org, June 13, 2006.

Holmes, Fred, "Bribery at Half a Million," *Badger Saints and Sinners,* E.M. Hale and Co., Milwaukee, 1939, 153–72.

"Railroad Land Grants Cause of State's Greatest Scandal," *Wisconsin State Journal,* Sept. 17, 1922.

Report of the Joint Select Committee Appointed to Investigate into Alleged Frauds and Corruption in the Disposition of the Land Grant by the Legislature of 1856, May 13, 1858.

Wisconsin Historical Society, *Dictionary of Wisconsin History,* www.wisconsinhistory.org/dictionary.

CHAPTER 5, "A HORRID DREAD": THE UNSOLVED MURDER OF H. C. MEAD

Johnson, June, *The Headless Banker—The Murder of Banker H. C. Mead as Waupaca Saw It,* Appleton, Wis.: PrintCource Plus, 2001.

———, Interview with Michael Bie, November 11, 2010.

Lynch, Russell, "One of Seven Still Survives," *Milwaukee Journal,* June 16, 1929.

"The Terrible Fate of H.C. Mead at Waupaca, Wis," *New York Times,* October 10, 1882.

Wisconsin Historical Society, *Dictionary of Wisconsin History,* "Joseph V. Quarles 1843–1911," www.wisconsinhistory.org.

CHAPTER 6, "PLASTER JOHN": THE MIRACLE HEALER OF SOMERSET

Dunn, James Taylor, "The 'Plaster Doctor' of Somerset," *Wisconsin Magazine of History*, Summer 1956, 245–50.

"John Till and His Miracle Plaster," Wisconsin Historical Society Odd Wisconsin Archive, www.wisconsinhistory.org/odd/archives/002761.asp.

"John Till: Was Barron County's Plaster Doctor a Huckster or a Healer?" Chippewa Valley Museum, www.cvmuseum.com/Till.

CHAPTER 7, THE LIFE AND CRIMES OF PIRATE CAPTAIN DAN SEAVEY

Boyd, Dr. Richard, "The Giant and the Pirate," Wisconsin Underwater Archeology Association newsletter Vol. 16, No. 3, September 2006.

Duchaine, William, "Two Fisted 'Pirate' Is Lake Port Legend," *Milwaukee Journal*, February 17, 1963.

Franz, Veronica, "Pirates on the Great Lakes," *Wisconsin Maritime Museum Anchor News*, Fall 2005.

"Pirate Caught on Great Lakes," *Chicago Tribune*, June 30, 1908.

Powers, Tom, *Michigan Rogues, Cutthroats & Desperadoes*, Friede Publications, Davison, MI, 2002.

"Seavey Funeral to Be Conducted on Friday," *Marinette Eagle*, February 15, 1949.

"Shot Stops a Lake 'Pirate,'" *New York Times*, June 30, 1908.

Stonehouse, Frederick, *Great Lakes Crime*, Avery Color Studies Inc., 2004.

"The Many Tales of Pirate Dan Seavey," *Marquette Monthly*, October 2008.

CHAPTER 8, VALLEY OF THE MOLLS

"County Jail is 'Honeymoon Hotel' to Gangster Girl," *Capital Times*, April 26, 1934.

"Dillinger Gang Girls in County Jail Here Under Heavy Guard," *Capital Times*, April 24, 1934.

"Dillinger Gang Molls Behind Bars Here," *Wisconsin State Journal*, April 24, 1934.

"Dillinger Girls Go Shopping, Drink Beer, Leave Our City," *Capital Times*, May 27, 1934.

Federal Bureau of Investigation, "John Herbert Dillinger," www.fbi.com.

"5,000 Join in Wide Search for Dillinger," *Capital Times*, April 26, 1934.

"Gang Girls Crack Under Grilling; Reveal Secrets," *Wisconsin State Journal,* April 26, 1934.

"Girls Here for U.S. Grand Jury," *Wisconsin State Journal,* April 25, 1934.

"Molls Under $150,000 Bail," *Capital Times,* April 25, 1934.

"Posse Hunts Nelson Near City, Fear Attempt to Free Bride From Jail Cell," April 30, 1934.

"3 Girls, Seized in Dillinger Raid, Freed on Probation," *Capital Times,* May 25, 1934.

Toland, John, *The Dillinger Days,* New York: Random House, 1963, 261–294.

CHAPTER 9, DOOMED: THE WINTER DANCE PARTY OF 1959

Amburn, Ellis, *Buddy Holly: A Biography.* New York, NY: St. Martin's Griffin, 1995.

Botsford, Joe, "It was crazy . . . a fine blast," *Milwaukee Sentinel,* January 24, 1959.

Buddy Holly Center, www.buddyhollycenter.org.

Lehmer, Larry, *The Day the Music Died: The Last Tour of Buddy Holly, the Big Bopper and Ritchie Valens,* Music Sales Group, 2004.

The Official Community of Buddy Holly, www.buddyholly .com.

"Snowstorms grip Midwest with Arctic cold to follow," *Milwaukee Journal,* January 22, 1959.

Steuer, Mark, "A Night Before the Music Died," *Voyageur Magazine,* Winter/Spring 1993, pp 17–22.

CHAPTER 10, PANCAKES FROM SPACE

Bie, Michael, "Dazed and Amused," ClassicWisconsin.com, 2004.

"Flying Saucer Cake Analysis Convinces Joe of Authenticity," *Three Lakes News,* June 29, 1961.

"Flying Saucer's Crew Landed to Fill Jug, State Man Reports," *Milwaukee Journal,* April 23, 1961.

"Got 'Cakes' from Saucer Men Is Claim of Joe Simonton," *Three Lakes News,* April 27, 1961.

"Joe Simonton Regrets Telling of Saucer," *Three Lakes News,* May 4, 1961.

"'Santa Claus' Gets Backing in Story of Flying Saucer," *Milwaukee Journal,* April 24, 1961.

"Santa Simonton who got outer-space pancake, dies," *Vilas County News Review,* August 24, 1972.

Satran, Dan, "How About It?" *Three Lakes News,* April 27, 1961.

"Saucer Is Sighted at Lorbetski Farm," *Three Lakes News,* May 4, 1961.

CHAPTER 11, THE ENDURING MYSTERY OF LEO BURT

Bates, Tom, *RADS, The 1970 Bombing of the Army Math Research Center and the University of Wisconsin and Its Aftermath,* New York: HarperCollins, 1992.

Federal Bureau of Investigation Featured Fugitive—Leo Frederick Burt, www.fbi.gov/wanted/fugitives.

Seely, Ron, and Deborah Ziff, "40 years later, FBI still looking for suspected terrorist Leo Burt," *Wisconsin State Journal,* July 21, 2010.

"Sterling Hall Bombing Nearing 40th Anniversary," WISC-TV 3, Madison, www.channel3000.com, July 21, 2010.

Vanden Brook, Tom, "Hunt still on for '70 blast suspect," *USA Today,* August 14, 2005.

CHAPTER 12, BEERMAN: THE MOBSTER WHO MADE MILWAUKEE INFAMOUS

"Banded in the Mafia," *Milwaukee Sentinel,* July 18, 1987.

"Bomb Victim on Mob List," Milwaukee Journal, July 1, 1978.

Cano, Julio, "Doctor's advice to call 911 not heeded, report says," *Milwaukee Sentinel,* February 11, 1993.

Daley, Dave, "The sins of the father," *Milwaukee Sentinel,* May 19, 1996.

Griffin, Dennis, *The Battle for Las Vegas—The Law vs. the Mob,* Huntington Press, 2006.

Hall, Clark, Testimony Committee on the Judiciary Subcommittee on Crime, July 24, 1996.

Janz, Bill, "Reporters' paper trail on Balistrieri reaches its end," *Milwaukee Sentinel,* February 12, 1993.

———, "Tracking the city's most dangerous mobster," *Milwaukee Journal Sentinel,* June 19, 2005.

Lonardo, Angelo, Statement before the U.S. Senate Permanent Subcommittee on Investigations, 1988.

"Man Dies as Bomb Explodes in Car," *Milwaukee Journal,* June 30, 1978.

Nichols, Mike, "Balistrieri memorialized with quiet dignity," *Milwaukee Journal,* February 11, 1993.

Rowen, Roy, "The Bookkeeper who did his job too well," *Fortune Magazine,* November 10, 1986.

"Secrecy continues in death," *Milwaukee Sentinel,* February 9, 1993.

Stephenson, Crocker, "Ex-mob boss Balistrieri dies," *Milwaukee Sentinel,* February 8, 1993.

Wilson, Mike, "Family Feud." *St. Petersburg Times,* April 23, 2001.

CHAPTER 13, THE MYTH OF THE MARINETTE MERCENARY

Chardy, Alfonso, "'Friends' paid for contra flight," *Miami Herald,* October 8, 1986.

"Explosion over Nicaragua," *TIME,* April 23, 1984.

Hasenfus, Eugene, and Sally Hasenfus, Plaintiffs-appellants, United States Court of Appeals, June 15, 1992.

"Hasenfus: Nothing But the Fact," *Revista Envio,* Number 65, November 1986.

Jasperse, Patrick, "Hasenfus getting his day in court," *Milwaukee Journal,* July 24, 1990.

Marinette Eagle Star, October 8–December 23, 1986.

Lamke, Ken, "Hasenfus stays behind the scenes," *Milwaukee Sentinel,* July 20, 1998.

Serrill, Michael S., "Nicaragua: Shot out of the Sky," TIME .com, June 21, 2005.

CHAPTER 14, THE LA CROSSE SERIAL KILLER

Epstein, Reid, "La Crosse fears a killer, mayor admits," *Milwaukee Journal Sentinel,* April 17, 2004.

Jungen, Anne, "College student missing; Mississippi search possible," La Crosse Tribune, February 15, 2010.

———, "Four drunken males found near drowning site," *La Crosse Tribune,* February 23, 2010.

"Kondracki suggests barrier, cameras," *La Crosse Tribune,* April 20, 2004.

Larimer, Sarah, "Disbelief reigns after student's body recovered," *Milwaukee Journal Sentinel,* October 3, 2006.

Morgan, Betsy, and Kim Vogt, "Why we are 99.9% sure it is NOT a serial killer—a data based explanation," April 2004.

"Public still reacting to drownings forum," *La Crosse Tribune,* April 23, 2004.

Richmond, Todd, "Wis. drowning blamed on drinking, not killer," *Associated Press,* September 4, 2007.

———, "Wis. town struggles to prevent drowning," *Associated Press,* October 22, 2006.

Springer, Dan, "Chief sets meeting on river deaths," *La Crosse Tribune,* April 20, 2004.

———, "Community seeks solutions," *La Crosse Tribune,* April 23, 2004.

———, "Police chief quells rumors of serial killer; alcohol blamed in Dion's death," *La Crosse Tribune,* April 16, 2004.

"Student who drowned in La Crosse was intoxicated," *Associated Press,* February 19, 2010.

"Your Views: Readers see foul play in drownings," *La Crosse Tribune,* April 18, 2004.

INDEX

ABOUT THE AUTHOR

Green Bay native and lifelong Wisconsin resident Michael Bie writes about travel, history, and culture in the Badger State. A graduate of the University of Wisconsin-Stevens Point, his previous books include *It Happened in Wisconsin* (Globe Pequot Press, 2007). His writing is featured at www.classicwisconsin.com.